WAITING
for the
SAVIOR

Reflections of Hope

John H. Timmerman

InterVarsity Press
Downers Grove, Illinois

InterVarsity Press® is the book-publishing division of InterVarsity Christian Fellowship®, a student movement active on campus at hundreds of universities, colleges and schools of nursing in the United States of America, and a member movement of the International Fellowship of Evangelical Students. For information about local and regional activities, write Public Relations Dept., InterVarsity Christian Fellowship, 6400 Schroeder Rd., P.O. Box 7895, Madison, WI 53707-7895.

Cover photograph: Robert Cushman Hayes

ISBN 0-8308-1354-3

Printed in the United States of America ♾

Library of Congress Cataloging-in-Publication Data

Timmerman, John H.
    Waiting for the Savior: reflections of hope/John H. Timmerman
        p.   cm.
    Includes bibliographical references.
    ISBN 0-8308-1354-3 (alk. paper)
    1. Bible—Biography.   2. Bible—Devotional literature.   3. Hope—
Religious aspects—Christianity—Meditations.   I. Title.
BS571.T56   1997
220.9'2—dc21   97-12917
                                                                            CIP

19	18	17	16	15	14	13	12	11	10	9	8	7	6	5	4	3	2	1
12	11	10	09	08	07	06	05	04	03	02	01	00	99	98	97			

For Pat, who walks with me in faith,
and for my four children—
Jeffrey, Betsy, Tamara and Joel.
But especially for those dear friends
who helped me keep watch,
for their comfort and faith in me
during the worst of my illness—
a time when this book
was also first drafted: 9/1/95-2/1/96.

Introduction

The year 1968, although long past now, is still one I would like to forget, but can't help remembering. Perhaps you know what I mean. It could be any year, but it is marked by events in such a way that you feel the imprint in all the years that follow.

In that year of 1968 my wife, Pat, and I had only been married two years—still newlyweds for all that, and giddily in love—and I was well into graduate studies to prepare for my teaching career. But far on the other side of the world a war raged out of all sane control, and it cut ever more deeply into the orderly lives in this world of the United States. Sons, husbands, fathers, lovers—they received draft notices that swept them headlong into that peculiarly savage war. It seemed a land of the unknown and unhomed, and I was one of those many caught in the whirlwind.

One thing united us all—a deep, almost primitive longing to return whole. Our hope was simple. Technically it was to make it through the required year of service; sometimes it was to make it through one more night. Our yearning was for a comfort that would last.

Then too, while we yearned to be back on the side of the world that we had left behind, our wives, children, parents, girlfriends lived in a hope and yearning that matched our own. They waited, watching evening news broadcasts to see which bases were hit before they could fall asleep. Or they spent the night in restless waiting. They met in Overseas Wives Clubs. They worked and waited and kept watch. They kept the home alive so the hope would stay lit. They kept a place for us to come home to.

They yearned to have us back as we yearned to be back. It was a longing of the heart that sometimes capsized in tears. But then they fumbled for hope again and tried to keep the fire lit.

The fear, of course, was that one or the other would not make it.

My point here is not to relive the particular fears and hopes of that war or that time. Rather, I believe the example touches on something universal to humanity. It is so fundamental to the nature of humanity, in fact, that it defines humanity itself. Not only in 1968 but in all times, we have a deep yearning for loving companionship, for a safe place to call home, for a deep intimacy with someone who can and will cradle our pain, accept our hurt, forgive our wrong, and who still wants us to come—just as we are. It is a yearning satisfied finally and only by God.

Clearly, no earthly treasure satisfies this action of the heart. On the contrary, the pursuit of earthly treasures twists the yearning into knots of anxiety. Nonetheless, it remains one of the marks of this age of relentless hurry, of instant gratification and insistence on physical results for time expended, that people avoid the source of true satisfaction. God is rejected as too remote to be relevant, too abstract to be real. And so this age substitutes pale imitations for the true comfort and erects mere skeletons in place of the living God.

The substitutions sought in this world cannot disguise, and cannot satisfy, the yearning for something more, something better, than this world has to offer.

If we look about us at this secularized world today, we might be quick to deny this yearning. In fact, we might observe two startling patterns as we look close. First, there are those people who seem wonderfully content in their own achievement. They have fulfilled, sometimes surpassed, the goals they have set for themselves. And if we confront our own hearts in a moment of candor, we might have to confess to an envy of their worldly splendor. Their yachts surpass our canoes; their cars are shinier than our clunkers. But, second, it also seems an age where hearts have turned to stone, where individuals live in isolated little cocoons of self-interest and could, apparently, care less about anything beyond this life. Truly, some have practiced the rigors of denial of yearning so long and so thoroughly that they seem to have perfected it. Their hearts of stone can't be cracked.

In each instance, however, it is more fitting to say that this deep, unquenchable yearning has been displaced or misplaced. People *displace* it when they pursue the physical allurements of this world. They govern their lives—and satisfy their longing—by what they can measure: a salary increase, a stock profit, possessions, their status in a consumer age. Nonetheless, the yearning is there. It feeds on its own coals, and is never satisfied.

In much the same way many people *misplace* their yearning, this passion for some way of life that seems better than their present one. They recognize that mere objects, the quantitative achievements of one's work, provide little lasting satisfaction. Their new car, after all, will soon be an old car. Their stock might fall in price as easily as rise. These people may turn inward, wrapping themselves in protective shells. But the more daring among them might also look outward for some source in which to place their hope, something that might satisfy the spiritual passion that refuses to be buried. Sometimes they look to Jesus. Increasingly in our age, however, they look instead to all the bewildering, strange religious cults, sects and groups that promise them peace in exchange for their lives and loyalty. In turning to this offer of inner peace, they turn from a Savior who gave *his* life for them.

Whether they displace or misplace their yearning, people of our age are drowning in hopelessness. We need a hope restored. We need to yearn with a passionate desire for intimacy with God. Even while we receive the touch of his grace here on this distant land we call earth, we long for the freshness and fullness of his grace to fall on us each day.

But if the modern age is drowning in hopelessness, it is not without a lifeline. We are not alone in watching and waiting for a Savior, that one who gives us hope for this life and for life eternal. Surely the Bible is God's clearest testimony to this hope, for hope is its primary theme, seamlessly woven in and through every book.

Moreover, we find—over and over again—people in the Bible keeping watch for the Savior, looking for their own lifelines of hope. They are so much like us—not all heroes, some on the point of despair. Some are just weary of the best, or indeed the worst, this world has to offer and yearn with a desperate intensity for a better way. Each of them kept watch for that better way. King David, Queen Esther, old Simeon, even Mary—these people and others discussed in this book kept watch, often when the night was dark and the way least clear. In them we find our own stories recreated. By finding parts of ourselves in them we also discover answers for our own waiting and hoping. They have walked where we now walk in our spiritual lives. Their lessons are our guides—chronicles of hope.

Above all, however, and this is also the goal of this book, they lead us to an end that beggars our imagination. Not only do we wait for the Savior; he waits for us. In fact, he is there all the time—in our joy or in sorrow, in despair or in certitude, he waits for us.

As we, like the biblical people in the chapters that follow, keep watch for the Savior, we hold fast to that certain hope: he is there in all of his intimate love, waiting to be found, ready to call out, "Welcome home, my child."

1

Shine like Stars
EVE

*I*T TURNED DARKER IN HER GARDEN THAT DAY.

Strangely, the luxuriant foliage that flung dew-rimmed light every which way blurred. Flowers that crept along the paths and played yellow and red games up the hillside now stooped as if with broken backs. And the blue bowl overhead held thickening clouds that cast shadows over the garden. Birds of prey wheeled.

It was a growing darkness. It came with the Deceiver's first sibilant hiss. He asked questions that shredded Eve's innocence, drawing incorrect conclusions from her correct responses. He bent the truth; no longer straight and firm, it wavered and fluctuated. The Deceiver pulled more tricks out of his magician's sack of deceptions. And, oh, the loveliness of his lie. Like any temptation since, it presented something first of all as good. It was pleasing. It was desirable (Genesis 3:6). This threefold action in Eve's heart under the sugary seduction of Satan is precisely the same strategy Satan employs today. We are lured into sin by thinking it is good. The more we look at it, the more pleasing it seems. Because it seems so very pleasing we want it. And the darkness falls.

It falls inside the soul, like the gray film that forms inside unwashed car windows. We can't see out clearly anymore. We are forced to look inward, and we realize that the darkness is our own loss of innocence.

So it happened to Eve and Adam. They saw the darkness falling for the first time. And the fear of the darkness, while Satan chuckled behind them, crept into Eve's heart like an infection, choking her, squeezing the last hope of innocence.

I know that feeling of panic. Suddenly my heart hammers in my throat, and I can't breathe. It comes over me at moments of intense fear or anxiety, when the realization floods over me that I am wholly inadequate to the problem before me. I feel it sometimes just before speaking to an audience, when I'm backstage nervously trying to pace off the feeling or hoping that it will somehow squeeze out of the soles of my shoes. But most often panic comes with the sudden, unavoidable awareness that I have done something wrong, all wrong. I have sinned. Then inside—hidden from others—nausea and tears ricochet off each other. I want to run, and to go on running until sheer exhaustion dissipates the tension.

Eve understood this feeling. With Adam she tried to sew fig leaves together to cover themselves, hands fumbling with the weavings. A desperate cover-up to deny the truth that lay in their hearts. And they knew it. They shrank deeper into the shadows then, afraid of the light. The damp recesses of the garden became their shelter. They tried to hide from God. Eve understood what they had done. And what they had lost. God had come to talk with them this evening in the garden. Remember that this was their custom of innocence, a tradition of pure friendship. It was like taking a walk with your beloved on a spring evening. But God didn't find them in the customary places. He had to call them out of their spiritual hiding to talk with them. And for any hope of restoration, Adam and Eve had to step out of hiding and meet with him.

It is a pattern as old as Eden. God still calls to us, huddled in our spiritual shadowlands. There can be no restoration of intimacy until we step out of the shadows, into his light.

The First Prophecy

When Eve stepped out, clothed in shame rather than naked in innocence, we can picture her averted eyes, her bowed head. There is a price to pay, of course; every sin, every violation of trust bears a consequence. Eve bore it, but so much seemed beyond her understanding simply because God's words were prophetic and future-oriented. Until that point they had no *need* for prophecy. No need to keep watch for deliverance.

Remember that Satan's presumed prophecy, "You will not surely die" (Genesis 3:4), was actually no prophecy at all. It was simply a lie from the master of lies. Then for the first time in history God provided a prophecy. He cursed the serpent, condemning it to crawl in the dust. Then he related the serpent to Eve in an earthshaking prophecy: "I will put enmity between you and the woman, and between your offspring and hers; he will crush your head, and you will strike his heel" (Genesis 3:15). Here at the dawn of human history, God announced the event for which hundreds of generations would keep watch. The head of the serpent Satan would be crushed, the authority of Jesus in this world would be clearly established, and the light that delivers us from the shadows would be given when Jesus died on the cross. Satan may have struck Jesus' heel in the crucifixion; Jesus crushed the power of Satan in the resurrection.

But the centuries rolled on. And the shadows thickened to darkness. The dark wings of Satan stretched their hideous shadow over the reaches of the globe. God's people seemed always looking, peering into the night sky. As they did so, the prophecies also grew stronger. Balaam prophesied: "I see him, but not now; I behold him, but not near. A star will come out of Jacob; a scepter will rise out of Israel" (Numbers 24:17). Did the people take comfort? *A star will come.* Or did they groan inwardly? *Not here. Not now.* How long do we have to wait for this star—this scepter-wielding Messiah—to take away our darkness? It is the very same question that riddles the hearts of so many of us.

Someone recently commented to me that the entire Old Testament could be looked upon as a night of impenetrable blackness. Occasionally one of these prophecies, like the very faintest pinprick, appears in the darkness. While I appreciated the point, I don't agree entirely with this extreme analogy. I disagree because even though humanity is fallen after Eden, God's grace has never failed. I disagree because even though sin's dark shadow covers the land, God sets the limits on the power and authority of that sin. He spoke to Moses from a burning bush. He led wayward Israelites by a pillar of fire. He touched Elijah's waterlogged altar into a blaze that set the prophets of Baal scurrying like frightened puppies.

I understand the concept of the Old Testament as a blanket of darkness if only because it resembles the darkness we ourselves feel. Truly, there are those times when God seems not like a pillar of fire leading us home, but like a distant pinprick in the night. As Eve walked from Eden, did she feel this way? Or was she able to affirm, *No matter how dark* this *night, I know he is there. I* have *walked with him in the garden.*

I believe Eve was white-knuckled with grief that first day east of Eden. Her soul wept for the comfort of God, and her heart yearned for the intimacy of his touch. But I do not believe that the darkness before her was without light, nor that she was wholly bereft of God's presence. Instead of despair in the night, Eve kept watch for the dawn.

In 1968 when I was separated from my wife and other loved ones by service in Vietnam, letters were my lifeline to home. Sometimes they were delayed for days, and I would wonder if I had been forgotten. Then one morning there would be a packet of seven or eight letters and maybe a package of home treats too. Still, I longed for a closer touch. I wanted to talk to someone who would speak back. It was then that I discovered the Military Affiliated Radio System (MARS).

The technical process, as far as I'm able to understand it, went something like this: radio-generated signals in Vietnam were intercepted by a ham radio operator in the United States and patched into a telephone connection. In theory this is fine, but in practice the two times I could reach a MARS station, it left much to be desired. First, you had to get to the station, usually buried in a bunker, where a telephone receiver hung from a wooden wall. Since the time zones were twelve hours apart, this took place generally between five to eight o'clock in the evening. The operator in Vietnam raised a radio receiver in the U.S., and the connection was established.

What followed was something like a mad comedy. Through a dense snarl of static buzz and blips, sometimes with other radio messages cutting in and out, and then with time lapses for the voice travel, I and my wife would try to pour out in words the feelings we hadn't been able to express for months. And then, all too quickly, it was time for the soldier behind me, and I shouted the last "I love you" into the phone and it was time to go.

I prefer to view the Old Testament as a series of MARS calls instead of as a dense blackness. At times the interference of the fallen world nearly drowns out the connection, but always, always, God is at the other end waiting to hear our desperate "I love you."

Nor is it totally different in today's world. Often our prayer lifeline is like that call. We squeeze a call out of our harried lives. And we long for a clearer connection. As the Old Testament becomes ever more clear to us in its chronicles of hope through people keeping watch for a savior, so too our keeping watch clarifies our hope.

For us the hope has come; the darkness has lifted. It is like the scene I witnessed this autumn morning as I prepared to write. A fog bank as thick and low as a herd of sheep lay over the eastern meadow. Behind the stand of empty maples, hickory and birch the orange edges of the sun shouldered upward. Here and there a random willow held dark leaves against its rising. And then the light touched the ground, and the fog bank twisted and separated and the whole meadow lay with a shining golden glow. The trees that a moment before looked like dark skeletons seemed transformed into a low hedge of tropical orchids, limbs and leaves touched with sparkling light.

On such a morning one can . . . almost . . . imagine Eden being reborn, brightly shining just over the horizon.

Light from the Darkness

Perhaps this golden morning is closer to our experience. God shines with the splendor of the Bright and Morning Star, making all things new. But maybe, just maybe, some of us are still waiting in the night, searching for hope. As we look back once again at Eve's departure from the garden, maybe we can find some directions for our own searching. They are not lessons perceptible to Eve as she turned her eyes eastward; she was aware only of her loss. Nonetheless, we are in a position where we can also look to the east with her toward the rising light of God's new Eden, and find a greater revelation for our own lives.

Consider God's miracle of creation itself. It was a series of powerful actions over the entire cosmos that set this small globe of earth with a special stamp. Surprisingly, that stamp of God's design was also a series of separations. Light separated from the darkness, now called night. The firmament separated from the waters. Upon command, the waters separated to distinct areas apart from land. Then separate kinds of vegetation and animals issued forth. And then, separate from them all because he was made in the image of God, the Lord made man.

Curiously, after every act of creative separation, God pronounced it good. Only in the last act of creation, however, is there reservation. God said, "It is not good for the man to be alone; I will make a helper suitable for him" (Genesis 2:18). One more act of separation was required to perfect Eden—a helper made suitable to Adam because she was made from a rib separated from his own body. Truly they were one, but separate. Only out of the separation could there be a unity for Adam and Eve.

What was left when Eve left Eden? Well, a marriage for one thing, providing a comforter of her own kind to travel the hard way with her. This was a union touched by the hand of God, and something of that sacred touch, surely, lingered on it. While separated from the intimacy of the Garden, these separated people—Adam and Eve— were blessed with unity neither could have alone.

Nor, even when our personal night seems most thick, are we abandoned. At times God may seem distant, even wholly separate, but the story of Eve shows us that our fear of abandonment is met by a comforter. Our effort to hide our fears in a lonely web of shame is met by one who calls out to us and waits to listen.

I often wonder what tears Eve shed as she walked from the garden that day. Perhaps, she dared one backward glance, only to see her home guarded by the angel's flaming sword. But what tears did she shed? She was no longer young—not now, having obtained the knowledge of good and evil—but maybe she wept the tears of the young. Do you remember such tears? The scraped knee, the little boy lost, the hungry infant. They cry for comfort. So maybe Eve's tears were first of all for comfort, and that was why it was so important to have Adam at her side. How desperately Eve needed comfort. Tears grow in price every year; when we believe we can no long afford them we cry inside. We exact the coinage of our heart's pain. We weep inside, as if a cloud in there were being squeezed. Were these the tears that Eve, no longer young, shed that day?

No matter where Eve, or any one of us, hides our tears, God will find them.

This union with God even in the midst of discord and darkness isn't limited to the marriage analogy of Adam and Eve, however. Indeed, it applies to all true believers—married, single, divorced. The great analogy that Scripture gives us for the kingdom of God is that of the Bride and the Groom. God is finally our perfect lover, and it is he whom we will meet at the marriage feast.

If the first lesson from Eve is that there is a comforter in our darkness, one who seeks union with us, consider secondly the ambiguous prophecy made to Eve concerning a new enemy. There forever will be enmity between Eve and Satan, between Eve's offspring and Satan (Genesis 3:15). And Eve's offspring will crush Satan's head, even while Satan strikes his heel. But what offspring? Genesis 3:20 tells us that Eve "would become the mother of all the living." So, the second lesson is that ongoing conflict that has always nipped at the heels of humanity—the eternal struggle between good and evil, right? Well, yes. But right only as part of the story, for Eve was also the mother of all humankind, and the story is an ongoing one, an unfolding one. Like those pinpricks in the night of the Old Testament, or like the haze of dawn, it is a revelation growing clearer every day. To see this, look briefly at only a few of Eve's descendants and their increasing perception, their divine clarifying, of the prophecy to Eve.

Jump ahead several thousand years. Along the way we find people like Isaiah who prophesied that "the people walking in darkness have seen a great light; on those living in the land of the shadow of death a light has dawned" (Isaiah 9:2). Or people like Malachi who proclaimed that "the sun of righteousness will rise with healing in its wings" (Malachi 4:2). We don't have to look very hard. The Bible is threaded with such passages that call us from our darkness to a light that will shatter it. A star will blaze in the heavens that will drive the shadows of the Garden out to waste places. A sun shall rise with such healing in its wings that even the hideous wings of the Destroyer will shrink back in terror. The promise to Eve drew closer: his head shall be crushed for what he has done to you.

Through the centuries' darkness, God's people kept watch for a light. John must have felt the weight of that past on his shoulders as the Holy Spirit inspired him to write his Gospel. From his very first words, it is utterly unlike the other Gospels, with their concern for genealogy and facts. Instead of tracing the Messiah's lineage back to King David, John traces him to the dawn of time: "Through him all things were made; without him nothing was made that has been made" (John 1:3). In the creation of the Garden too? Yes, that too. And "in him was life, and that life was the light of men" (1:4). A light also to Eve and Adam, then, even while they crept through the shadows. And here is why, John adds, "The light shines in the darkness, but the darkness has not understood it" (1:5).

In Eve's darkness? And in mine?
In the darkness we fail to see clearly. It is like a night inside the walls

of our minds, and we grope for indicators of the safe way. The prophets gave many indicators as they reminded the people of the star that would blaze in the darkness or the sun that would arise with healing in its wings.

The signs, the directions, reminded the people how to live while keeping watch.

But here is the extraordinary thing, the most extraordinary thing in all history. For, as John testifies, the light came down and entered the people's darkness to search for them. Jesus himself identified himself as such: "I am the light of the world. Whoever follows me will never walk in darkness, but will have the light of life" (John 8:12).

One can imagine the demons in the shadows shifting. The promise to Eve was fulfilled on this earth one dusty night in Jerusalem. The demons must have gathered in those hours with all of Satan's tactical ploys. Subvert Judas and break Jesus' closest ranks. Round up the Pharisees, and let them be a posse of pride. It was working. The nails through Jesus' wrists, then through his ankles ("You will strike his heel"). The sky grew black at midday, and the light of life died on the cross.

But they couldn't forget the rest of the prophecy. It was not dying that the light defeated; it was death itself. On that resurrection morning when light exploded from the sepulcher, Jesus crushed the head of death itself. Get that verb right. He didn't just kick it around a bit or knock it aside: he *crushed* death. It is why Paul could proclaim, in 1 Corinthians 15, "Where, O death, is your victory? Where, O death, is your sting?" (v. 55). The star of the morning has risen.

The light has come; like a searchlight in the darkest night it has come. Sometimes its very brightness startles us. Sometimes it shows how very thin we are, how deeply we have hidden the darkness in our own hearts. Often the light seems to drill into the core of our spiritual selves. Like Eve we try to cover ourselves in clumsy fabrics. Sometimes the best we can stitch together is a frayed net of lies. So like Eve we shrink into the shadows.

For the believer, as with Eve at the voice of God, there is no hiding.

Peter tells us why in his epistle. This morning star we've talked about, this brilliant, comforting, but exposing light? It also dwells in the heart of the believer. It ignites a flame we carry into the world. Peter writes, "You will do well to pay attention to it, as to a light shining in a dark place, until the day dawns and the morning star rises in your hearts" (2 Peter 1:19). Comforting, but also a somewhat frightening thought that this morning star, looked for by people throughout the Old Testament, has come and now lives within our hearts.

Well, what do we do with it? Listen to Paul: "Do everything without complaining or arguing, so that you may become blameless and pure, children of God without fault in a crooked and depraved generation, in which you shine like stars in the universe as you hold out the word of life." (Philippians 2:14-16). Yes, shine like stars by holding out the word of life. In the same way that the light of life penetrates our shadows, so we break into the darkness of others.

But this life—our work here—is not the end of the story. It never is. For the things of this life will all pass away. They did for Eve. They did for those prophets peering so hard into the future. They did for the disciples—sometimes in gruesome ways—who so boldly proclaimed the message that burned like stars in their hearts. They will for us. Indeed, the stars of the heavens themselves will pass away, rolled up like a scroll. The dark shadowed sides of ourselves will be peeled clean and rolled away with them. But one thing will remain: "I, Jesus, have sent my angel to give you this testimony for the churches. I am the Root and the Offspring of David, and the bright Morning Star" (Revelation 22:16). Crossing over the River of Life, we leave all our darkness behind and enter the eternal city where we "will not need the light of a lamp or the light of the sun" (Revelation 22:5). Our light is from the bright Morning Star, the same who crushed the serpent's head, who is our light forever and ever and where no shadows can enter.

The Bible begins in a garden much like that city, a place where the Lord talked with his loved ones. From that first moment of deceit in the Garden, the shadows drew close, and God's loved ones have yearned from the darkness to talk with him in close communion.

That yearning is the subject of this book, for we have much to learn from the way biblical characters kept watch for Jesus. We sometimes tend to see them as rather remote, or superhuman, characters. Look at King David, with his fabulous wealth and storied kingdom. Beautiful Queen Esther—was her beauty only of appearance or of her heart?

Such are the characters we meet as we ourselves keep watch for the bright Morning Star. As we do so, we discover that they and we have so very much in common in our shadowlands. David may have had uncountable wealth, but his heart broke for a wayward son. And Esther? She didn't just flutter her beautiful eyelashes to save her people. She risked almost certain death. Little Mary, the country girl, risked the ridicule of kinfolk while holding the warmth of the Morning Star within her.

These people were tested, sometimes bitterly. They are not just superheroes of long ago; rather, they are very special guides to us in the present as we too keep watch for the Savior's light.

For Further Study

Read Genesis 3

1. What three traits of the fruit does Satan use to tempt Eve (see v. 6)?

2. How are they like any temptation to sin that we face?

3. What are the immediate consequences of sin for Adam and Eve? What feelings do we have when we sin? List the ways that Jesus responds to us.

4. Even though Adam and Eve had sinned and by God's standard of justice had to be punished, how does God show loving tenderness toward them (see vv. 15 and 21)?

5. What does it mean to say that Jesus crushed death (read 1 Corinthians 15:12-17, 42-49)?

Prayer

Lord, what was surely my eternal darkness you have shattered by the brilliance of Jesus' resurrection. Forgive my falling prey to Satan's deceit. Forgive my wanting to. Help me look to the light of your Word and will alone as I walk through this world east of Eden. Amen.

2

Out of the Depths
DAVID

*P*ICTURE THIS KING, A FABULOUSLY WEALTHY AND POWERFUL potentate, this man whose word commanded the lives of millions—picture him down on his knees pleading with God for help. There's the great paradox of King David. The greatest hero of Israel; the heartbroken human on his knees.

One Bible scholar described David as "that two-fisted lover," and then left the reader to decipher what he meant. Indeed, the ambiguities are endless. At one moment he reaches his hands out grasping for God; at the next he draws them to himself full of the lusts of his flesh. He has a wife who has left her mean-spirited husband to marry him; he himself is the mean-spirited husband who turns all his desire on the wife of another man. Worse, he has the man killed so he can fulfill the lusts that blaze like an inferno in his heart. And then . . . then he has the audacity to fall on his knees once again and ask God to renew the fires of his first love for him.

David is everything we despise and everything we admire. He is all too human; there is a bit of David in all of us. At one moment we love

David, and we also love ourselves, knowing we are beloved of God. At the next moment, we loathe David, as we sometimes loathe ourselves, knowing we have sinned against God.

There are human mysteries in King David—the disconsolate mysteries of the human heart. Yet we come back to this portrait—like an irreducible mathematical equation—of David on his knees. His is also the human heart longing for closeness to God, keeping faith and keeping watch for the benediction of God's coming into his life.

Many of David's songs, so many of which seem uttered from his knees, capture this longing with an intense, brutal power. And in so many of these the peace bringer, the One who draws close and comforts David's discomforted heart, is the great King, the Messiah. David longed for *Someone,* sent from God, bearing God's deliverance. It was not simply a deliverance from enemies and war, for David had experienced that in abundance. He had cried out to God about that, and God had responded in dramatic, earth-shaking ways. Rather, it was a seeking of deliverance for his own troubled soul.

How can we miss this divine irony of David's plea for deliverance? Out of the lineage of King David, the one who longed for the Deliverer, would come that Deliverer himself. They were knit by blood. So too it is for us as we walk the depths of our own trials. Out of our longing for deliverance, in response to it, the divine Deliverer comes. He comes not as some outside force, like an avenging general of some foreign army, but he comes like one near and dear to us. You may call him a blood relative to each one of us also. By his blood our deliverance comes.

Songs of Deliverance

The poems uttered by King David are, as C. S. Lewis put it in his essay "The Psalms," our spiritual "ancestors." Through the ages since their writing they retain the ability to strike forcibly, even "terribly," to the core of our spiritual reality. One reason for this, surely, is David's method of using metaphors, suggestive patterns that hint at a truth that endures for all time.

More than a thousand years before Jesus was born, David cried out for *Someone*. Certain only that that Someone existed and would appear, uncertain of who that Someone was or when he would appear, King David used figurative images to describe his Deliverer. In this way, certain psalms bear a deeper, more powerful, and future-enacted meaning than the mere words in their historical context suggest. Although the Messiah is mentioned by name in none of the Psalms, his nature and work, as later Jews and Jesus himself understood, are clearly foreshadowed.

The point here is not just a little academic detour. Consider this: if indeed the Psalms are, as C. S. Lewis argued, our spiritual ancestors, perfectly capturing our own emotional and spiritual struggles, and since Jesus indeed is the hereditary descendant of David and we are, as the Bible testifies, sons and daughters of Christ, then that places us very much in proximity to David himself. Not only in our mutual meeting in Jesus, but indeed in the very heart and soul of that troubled king, that two-fisted lover longing for a perfect love. Draw the picture together now. We stand with David in these psalms he crafted. We keep watch with him for the Deliverer. He voices our agony and despair. We look with him for a rock in a desert land, for that bit of shade that shelters us, for that living water that revives us again.

Put a human face on David's loneliness a moment. He was gifted by God with one of life's greatest treasures—a friend, Jonathan, who was so close to David's heart that he was indeed closer than a brother. I am awestruck by the power of David's love for Jonathan. It drives to the core of my—or anyone's—own need for a friend, not a mere acquaintance but one whose soul holds my own in trust. And then, by a whim of Jonathan's tyrannical father, King Saul, these two soulmates were forever ripped apart. The human picture here is of a deep friendship stamped into pieces by a blind human rage.

This fragileness of human relationships reminds me of another person in the twentieth century. Her name is Irina Ratushinskaya, and in this case she struggled for a relationship with God when her

God was denied and her friendships torn apart under the iron fist of communism in the then U.S.S.R.

Already at the age of ten, Irina was something of a rebel. As she sat in the schoolroom in her hometown of Odessa one day, looking out the window at flakes of snow in the air and enduring yet one more class in Atheism Instruction, Irina wondered why it was that the authorities—over and over—insisted there was no God. If there wasn't, what were they so afraid of? The little rebel, as she tells her story in her autobiography *In the Beginning,* decided to take God's side in the matter, knowing little, however, about God at all. So she put him to the test. It seldom snowed heavily in Odessa. These flakes were rare. Yet, with her ten-year-old audacity, Irina asked God that, if he were real, he would make it keep snowing.

Over the next few days Odessa received one of the heaviest snowfalls it had ever recorded.

To be a Christian during the oppressive cruelty of the Kruschev regime was to be an alien in one's own homeland. In fact, Irina did not come across a Bible, finally given to her by a Jewish friend, until she was twenty-three. But just as her faith was maturing by reading the Scripture, the most deliberately coordinated oppression of Christians was being used by Kruschev's successor, Leonid Brezhnev, and his powerful ally, the KGB. It was easy for them to target Irina and her dissident husband, Igor Geraschenko. She was arrested on September 17, 1982, charged with the crime of anti-Soviet agitation. The evidence? Her poetry. The sentence? Seven years hard labor and five years internal exile.

Here is where I see the heart of David still beating in this woman, Irina Ratushinskaya. She was torn from her husband by a power she could not resist. She was abandoned to a freezing cell in the Barashevo Labor camp (for "especially dangerous state criminals"), subjected to beatings, terrible illness and long periods of solitary confinement in a cramped cell. How often, I wonder, did she cry out like David? Friendless. Abandoned.

But not altogether. She still had her poems, which she scratched into a bar of soap with a burnt match and then memorized, eventually smuggling them out on scraps of paper. In one she writes, "They've taken my friends,/ripped the cross from its chain." In these scraps her love and her faith beat on strongly. How does one measure such courage, such faith? It literally makes me shiver when I try to place myself in Irina's freezing cell.

But grace, as it did in David's life, also penetrated the bleakness of Irina's Barashevo cell. One of my favorite of her poems, a quiet and humorous one, tells how she was given a special friend while in solitary confinement. She called it—this small mouse—her fellow political prisoner. And there was further grace. Irina was released on the eve of the Reykjavik summit between Reagan and Gorbachev, and allowed to go to London for medical treatment. She was reunited with her husband, and there they have built a new life.

People like King David and Irina Ratushinskaya have wrestled desperately with those moments when their lives seemed to lie in ruins. Perhaps few of us have endured the profound abandonment that they did. It is far more likely, however, that nearly any one of us can share the sense of spiritual anguish they endured.

David often wrestled with this despairing anguish in which he felt forsaken and in need of deliverance. In Psalm 130:1 he raises this plea, "Out of the depths I cry to thee, O LORD." The depths are a miserable place. Some of us have spent a long time there, wondering, out of a fog of darkness and uncertainty, when a light will come. Perhaps some of us too, like David, have wandered in the depths because of a wayward child. We have kept the night watch, waiting for that child, listening for the car in the street or the footsteps on the porch, while the long minutes slowly tick away. We too have lived in the depths, longing for our Absalom to come home. Is it any wonder that we who have wandered in the depths find our spirits devouring David's promises? Psalm 147 promises us that the Lord "heals the brokenhearted and binds up their wounds," and we long for healing of our own riven hearts. Psalm 91 tells us that the Lord "will command his angels concerning you to guard you in all your ways," and we in the depths want to feel the brush of those wings of power over our kneeling bodies. And when David cries out in Psalm 61, "Hear my cry, O God; listen to my prayer," those of us who have beat on the doors of heaven with our prayers also feel, like David, that "I call as my heart grows faint," and that we need to be led "to the rock that is higher than I."

All the emotions of human living—*our* human living—are poured into these songs of David, from rapturous joy over God's creative splendor to the wrenching anguish of being mired in the depths. Is it any wonder we feel close to David?

But David also anticipates a response to his heart-driven pleas. He doesn't hang them out on some prayer line to blow in the wind. He knows, he insists, that the Lord God hears these prayers and is shaping a response to them even as he prays. David's God is a Lord of action, not some sedentary, reflective figure who haunts Eastern religions like a sublime abstraction. This God, our God, *acts.*

And so David is right to expect deliverance. He anticipates healing for the brokenhearted, he foresees uplifting by the angels of heaven, he insists that when his heart grows faint, God will lead him to that higher Rock. And down through the centuries he sees the Deliverer who is Jesus.

Who the Deliverer Is

Several of David's psalms make this foreseeing absolutely specific. They anticipate the office of this Deliverer; that is, as the Messiah. These psalms determine who this Deliverer is.

Psalm 2 captures David's two-way vision as he focuses on the present moment and longs for a moment to come. The psalm was likely composed for the coronation of later kings, invoking the Lord's help for "his Anointed One." The king was in fact anointed with oil as a sign of his installation to a holy office. Two things, however, stand out in particular importance in the second verse of the psalm. First, the Anointed One is closely, intimately allied with the Lord, so close that to rebel against one is to rebel against the other; to love and serve the one is to love and serve the other. At David's time that Anointed One would be the king, acting in his office as God's agent. Second, that very term, *Anointed One,* bears significance, for the Hebrew word used is *Messiah* (the Greek word for "Anointed One" is *Christ*). This is the term that the prophets would use as they kept watch for the coming Anointed One. It is also the term Matthew uses (1:17) to identify the office of Jesus. So too David looks ahead to a special kind of king—one who is God incarnate.

Similarly, Psalm 72, another song suited for coronation ceremonies, adds definition to who this Redeemer is. This psalm identifies the Messiah as "the royal son," who is righteous and just (vv. 1-2). His rule will be an eternal rule, not just for one lifetime (v. 5). His reign will extend not just over Israel, but to the ends of the earth (vv. 8-11). Moreover, this Messiah will be a Deliverer of his people, one showing great compassion and pity (vv. 12-14). This psalm, with others such as Psalm 110, became a source guide for such later prophets as Isaiah, Jeremiah and Zechariah as they looked for the Messiah, and the early church took it as a clear application to Jesus.

In such a way, David defines who this Messiah *is.* He is righteous and just. He will rule eternally. And he will deliver his people through his great compassion and pity for them. Moreover, a constant thread throughout the Psalms also comes together in a whole portrait of what this Messiah will *do.*

What the Deliverer Will Do

There is this to be said about David. Although he was a hot-blooded sinner, he also *knew* he was a sinner and desperately longed for purification. It is not always that way with sinners—for which we can also read all humanity. We have such subtle defense mechanisms, such clever denials that can become life patterns. We give ourselves easy grace . . . "Father, forgive me . . . " For what, though? And sometimes our own sense of spiritual certitude, when it hardens into self-righteousness, can be our worst sin. The bad word *sanctimoni-*

ous, after all, stands like a wall against the good word *sanctification.* There is little room in the kingdom of God for smug self-sufficiency.

David knew better. In Psalm 51, he lays the reality of his sin directly on the line: "I know my transgressions, and my sin is always before me. Against you, you only, have I sinned and done what is evil in your sight" (vv. 3-4). No wonder he longs for a Redeemer. And in the confession of his sinfulness, he finds one. Here is the rest of his prayer-song: "Cleanse me with hyssop, and I will be clean; wash me, and I will be whiter than snow" (v. 7). Later prophets latched on to this verse eagerly (see Isaiah 1:18; Daniel 7:9). They too kept watch for the Messiah as Redeemer, the deliverer from our sins.

One of the keys to the fullness of this expectation lies in that common Judean herb, the hyssop. From earliest times this common plant bore special ceremonial significance for cleansing. The earliest mention of it occurs in Exodus 12:22, where God directs the people to dip hyssop in blood and to strike the doorposts and lintels as a sign of protection and purity during the Passover. The angel of death passed them by. Similarly, in Leviticus 14:4, 6 and 52, hyssop is used in the ceremony of cleansing for lepers. Thus the plant bears a powerful symbolism for cleansing in the Hebrew kingdom (the Hebrew word for "cleanse" literally means to *un-sin*), and surely David's reference to it evokes that powerful symbolism.

The significance of the plant does not end there with David however, for the hyssop plant also bears powerful significance for Jesus. As he hung on the cross, his body parched in the Judean heat, his thirst overpowering as body fluids began to collect in his chest cavity, Jesus called out, "I thirst." And, as John 19:29 records it, his executioners extended to him a vinegar-dipped sponge on the end of a branch of hyssop. Of course mockery lay in the very act; the bitterness of the vinegar to a thirsty man was very much like the bitterness of Jesus' dying to cleanse us from our sin. Here, on the cross, Jesus enacted the purification of human sin.

A second major theme in David's psalms concerning what this Redeemer will do points to the triumphant act of Jesus' resurrection, for here too David keeps watch for life eternal. The theme, in fact, provides a hope after the depths, and it plunges David headlong into a celebration of joy.

Eternal life and joy—the two go inextricably together. In our certain expectation of life eternal lies our joy. Our lives may not always be happy on this earth, but they will explode into joy in the new heaven and earth. This expectation, however, ignites a flicker of joy in this life even when we struggle in the depths.

Psalm 16 dramatically outlines the expectation. It is uttered out of the depths, to be sure, as it voices a plea for safety. "Keep me safe, O God," David begs in the first verse, "for in you I take refuge" (v. 1). It must have seemed to David at times that his life was a never-ending war. Sometimes he praises God for victory and gives thanks that the Lord "has trained his hands" for battle.

David was beset by warfare from without, and pleaded for protection against death. I have served during a time of war and know well David's prayer. But the battlefield is only one kind of warfare for the Christian. We are under persistent attack by powers and principalities, a truth set forth by Paul: "For our struggle is not against flesh and blood, but against the rulers, against the authorities, and against the powers of this dark world" (Ephesians 6:12).

In his book *The Bondage Breaker* (Harvest House, 1993) Neil Anderson provides an answer to this persistent attack: "Demons gain access to our lives through our points of vulnerability. Yet we are not to care what Satan thinks of us; we are to live our lives in a way that is pleasing to God" (p. 104). Therein lies our safety, and the safety David prayed for—living in the Lord's will and trusting his deliverance. How desperately some of us, having experienced betrayal by friends or loved ones whom we trusted, need to keep watch for that safe place of God's arms. There no confidence is broken, no hand turns us away, no laughter rings in our ears. He calls us: O my Child.

David was delivered, time after time, from the shadow of death and the horrors of warfare. David knew that death could not be *escaped*. But it would be *overcome*. Just as the Lord had delivered him from human warfare, so too, David insists, the Lord will deliver him from that final warfare with death. This life is not the end of the matter; there is a life to come where the Lord will be the light of peace among his people. David testifies that because the Lord "is at my right hand, I will not be shaken" (Psalm 16:8). On that premise he declares: "My heart is glad and my tongue rejoices; my body also will rest secure, *because you will not abandon me to the grave,* nor will you let your Holy One see decay" (Psalm 16:9-10).

David uses that term "Holy One" which once again provides us with a two-way vision. Surely David refers to himself as the anointed king. Surely he does not refer to any personal merit, all too well aware as he is of his own sin. But surely also the name anticipates that mighty, earth-shattering act of the Holy One, Jesus, who stood death on its head in his resurrection. Because that Holy One lives, we too will live.

The glory of the Psalms sings in our ears, but they carry only part of the full song. In 1 Corinthians 13 Paul writes that we see in part, as if in a cloudy mirror. So too was David's vision. In his case, however, it was like a telescope trained not across a thousand miles of space but through a thousand years of time. What he saw was 100 percent accurate, but still only part of the whole. Little did he know that the Messiah would turn the world upside down.

Jesus, born in the lineage of the very king who so earnestly kept watch for him, looks backward frequently to quote that same king. Each time it is like a punctuation mark: I am the Messiah. I am the one for whom David kept watch. In the debate with the Pharisees recorded in Matthew 22, Jesus uses David's words to show the precedence of the Messiah over the earthly king: "How is it then that David, speaking by the Spirit, calls him [Christ] 'Lord'? For he says, 'The Lord said to my Lord: "Sit at my right hand until I put your enemies under your feet." ' If then David calls him 'Lord,' how can he be his son?" (vv. 43-45). Similarly, in his discourses to the people or his disciples, Jesus frequently includes quotations from Davidic psalms in his comments.

That biblical unity between King David and Jesus is as powerful as the roots of God's omnipotent plan for all creation. It is nearly unimaginable to us. It is as if I said, "I desperately need a deliverer," and a thousand years from now someone in my direct lineage became that deliverer.

But I need not say that. For me, the Deliverer *has* come. I am in *his* very lineage. I am a son of Christ the Redeemer, as is any brother or sister of mine who claims our unity by the redemption of Jesus. They may say with me, "I am a child of the Great King, the Most High Lord. When I slog through the depths, I know that he will deliver me. When I feel joy like a fountain in my soul, I let it overflow in praise. And when I am threatened, I will not be afraid. My Redeemer has arms that will hold me and never push away."

The great power for us lies in the way the Psalms situate us in looking for Jesus. With David we keep watch, from the depths or from the moment of rejoicing. But we have met the Savior. This Anointed One has come; this Deliverer and Redeemer has done his precious work for us. This Conqueror of Death stands with us in his resurrection power. Our watch too has been fulfilled by his coming, and our faith met by his eternal reality.

For Further Study

Read 1 Samuel 13:13-14; 16:7

1. David is described as a man after God's own heart. What does that mean in ideal terms? What does it mean practically, given the state of human nature?

2. How is David—and the events of his life—an embodiment of this conflict between the ideal and the human reality of everyday practice?

3. Describe how this conflict between the ideal and the human reality arises in your own life. Think of concrete examples. What do *you* do with them?

4. Consider those ways David deals with his sin and despair. What lessons emerge for us? Read Psalm 51. What specific steps of reconciliation are outlined, and what affirmations are made?

5. Describe the difference between the terms *sanctimonious* and *sancti-*

fication as used in this chapter. Give concrete examples of how these two terms may work in a Christian's life. What are the effects of either one?

6. How do the Psalms relate to your personal relationship with Jesus? Locate one in particular that does this.

Prayer

I'm afraid—truly afraid—that I am no different than David. I long for a holy heart that feels close to you. Yet so often I feel only the hollowness of separation that I myself have carved out of our relationship, Lord. Restore me, I pray. Be my Rock and Redeemer, my quickening spring in a dry and thirsty land, so that I might drink deeply of your Spirit and draw close to you again. Amen.

3

Perfect Peace
ISAIAH

WITHIN TWO HUNDRED AND FIFTY YEARS OF HIS REIGN, David's vision of the peaceable kingdom under the rule of God was like dust in the wind.

The kingdom itself fractured in two—Israel and Judah. In a few generations the ruling kings were scarcely different from any political potentates of the time. They were greedy for self-glory. They celebrated any pagan religious festival that brought immediate gratification. Wanton sexuality rampaged where once there was spirituality. Waiting on the Lord became a mere idea, rather than a practice. If remembered at all, it was associated with those tired leaders of ages past, a mere anachronism. Time now to get on with it—party hard, enjoy what can be enjoyed and bury belief in the graveyard of history.

By the middle of the eighth century B.C. the internal collapse of the peaceable kingdom also brought external threat. Arrayed like a mighty cordon, ready to tighten and squeeze the life out of Israel and Judah, stood the fierce Assyrian armies. They massed by the thousands to the north, about to sweep the land like an avenging wind. To the south stood the desolation of the desert. In between cowered God's chosen people, but a people who had chosen against God. They had forgotten the first things; now they had nothing left but the bitterness of their own hedonistic lifestyles. It was an evil time in this desert of unbelief.

Among God's chosen people, however, stood some individuals particularly designated by God to keep watch in the dry places, to clarify the muddled spiritual water, to point the way to a fountain of new life.

Peace in a Troubled Time

It is sometimes hard for us moderns to keep in mind the historical pattern of Isaiah's time. And it's little wonder. With the rapid change of kings, times of brief but urgent reform and periods of deep spiritual pollution, the history from David to Isaiah was frenzied and disordered. Perhaps in this respect Israel's history was not altogether different from ours.

To summarize, using the most reliable current dating, here's what happened. After the death of King Saul, David ruled the united kingdom from 1010 to 970 B.C. and was succeeded by his son Solomon. After the death of Solomon in 930, the formerly united kingdom split into the northern kingdom of Israel and the southern kingdom of Judah. For the next two hundred years these kingdoms coexisted, often in bitter conflict with each other, and each competing with abandon in acts of evil.

Isaiah, the first of the great or so-called major prophets, lived in Judah from about 765 to 681. Micah was a contemporary of Isaiah in Judah; Amos and Hosea near contemporaries in Israel. During that time, in the year 722, the northern kingdom of Israel fell to the Assyrians, who would later fall to the Babylonians. Thus the threat to Judah when Isaiah began his prophetic ministry, generally dated from 735 when King Uzziah died, was immediate and real. But not nearly as urgent, declared Isaiah, as the threat to the spiritual lives of God's people.

About Isaiah himself we are told little. Bits and pieces of historical facts and pictures filter down to us, many of them, however, colored by the speculations of later commentators and historians. We do know that he was married to a prophetess, which should be, understood not as the wife of a prophet, but, like Miriam, Deborah and Huldah, a prophet in her own right. We also know that, like some later prophets (Elijah, John the Baptist), he wore a garment of haircloth or sackcloth. And one long-standing tradition has it that Isaiah met death by being sawn in two by the wicked king Manasseh. It is surely clear that Isaiah ministered in a troubled time, and brought a message of perfect peace that he was willing to die for. That is the dramatic spiritual history of this keeper of the watchtower of faith.

Appropriate for his time, but no less for ours, Isaiah brings a message of peace emerging out of terror and uncertainty. In the depths of our deepest fears, peace seems impossibly remote; we can hardly remember what it is like. At such times we need someone to pour encouragement into our ears and heart. When we can't feel it, we need more than ever to *believe* it. We need someone to insist with granitic certainty that God's "perfect peace" is with us, that even though we walk through the rivers of desolation or through the fires of temptation and deceit, God walks with us, closer than ever. We need someone to testify that at our loneliest hour, when the world has battered our hearts into weakness, God draws close to hold us with his victorious right hand.

Isaiah, prophet of peace, was such a one.

Isaiah's Message of Peace

While the longing for the Messiah plays strongly, like some exquisite melody, throughout Isaiah's prophetic writings, three major themes also emerge: we are sinful, we need to recognize our need for redemption, and we have a Savior.

Our greatest immediate need couldn't be clearer: redemption from our sins. The situation in Isaiah's time differs little from our own in this regard. Sin assaulted the people and distorted their lives more powerfully than any foreign army. Their idols of wood and stone may differ from ours of money, power or sex, but the *impulse* toward these idols remains constant over the course of the centuries. Humanity has turned from God to pursue fallen human desire. As with Isaiah's people, we too desperately need a Redeemer.

That is Isaiah's first great prophecy. There is a Savior. He is at hand and able to deliver us. This grand theme opens the book like a triumphant proclamation; it continues unabated until the closing vision of the peaceable kingdom that lasts forever.

After his opening call to the people in chapter 1, Isaiah announces the Lord's request: "Come now, let us reason together," says the LORD. "Though your sins are like scarlet, they shall be white as snow; though they are red as crimson, they shall be like wool." This loaded little verse summarizes the charge against and the hope for the people. They have been unreasonable; following their own way into self-gratification and the dangerous game of political intrigue, the people have forsaken the reasonable order of a godly life. It makes no sense.

Isaiah must have been shaking his head as he looked out over a sea of human folly and watched the people foundering in the very sea they had created. "Why do you persist in rebellion?" he asks. "Your whole head is injured" (Isaiah 1:5). The charge brings to mind a picture of a parent chastening a wayward child on the playground: "Look, I warned you not to jump from the top of the monkey bars." Like children, we as human beings more often choose to disregard such warnings. And at such times we need to be told, quite firmly and authoritatively, that we are acting unreasonably. Through Isaiah, God calls the people back to reason; we have a desperate need to be forgiven our sins.

Am I Unreasonable?

Anyone can recall dozens of instances of unreasonableness occurring around us. The international political scene today bears eerie resemblances to Isaiah's time. Nation rises against nation. Armies move in the smoke and debris of missiles and mortars to take more land, only to lose it again, and the land itself is blasted into a gray moonscape of infertility.

Many churches are fractured by ecclesiastical unreasonableness. Fellowship degenerates in direct proportion to the level of raised voices. Personal agendas are set forth like absolute truths; personal beliefs raised to a par with Scripture, perhaps even superseding it. In her winsomely delightful novel *Saint Maybe* (Knopf, 1991), Anne Tyler conveys such an unreasonableness of ecclesiastical dissent. The good Reverend Emmett has founded the Church of the Second Chance for those people who want a new religious start, who feel alienated from the mainline church and who want to live according to strong moral values. But, like Isaiah, Reverend Emmett has to call them back to first things. He laments, "There's so much I've looked away from. I see everyone has made Second Chance his own, adapted it to suit his own purposes, changed the rules to whatever is more convenient, and I pretend not to notice" (p. 259).

You don't have to search long to find dozens of personal instances of unreasonableness. I recall when I was a new—and very young— deacon in our church in Pennsylvania. I wanted to be a good deacon, to call regularly on every member in my district. The trouble was Mrs. Dottlemeyer (not her real name), a widow of about seventy-five, who lived only two blocks away in a neat, small house. Amazingly, her visitation card showed not one contact in over ten years.

Well, I'd get busy on that.

The first time I went I took along an Easter lily. The door opened a crack, a small hand slipped through, snatched the lily, and the door slammed shut. Hard.

That first visit didn't stop me, though. I went twice more that spring, dressed nicely, trying my best to look nonthreatening. When she peeked through the door window, I called out, "I'm from the church." But she disappeared back into her narrow little house.

One evening I was lamenting to my wife how *unreasonable* Mrs. Dottlemeyer was being. "Maybe she's just scared of men," said Pat.

"Isn't that unreasonable?" I asked. "I'm not scary."

"Look," she said. "I'll bake her something and go with you."

A few days later we all arrived at her door, Pat and I and our two toddlers, along with some soup and baked goods. Magically the door opened. Mysteriously we had a wonderful visit. It was the first of many. In fact, when Mrs. Dottlemeyer had to move into a nursing home, she called Pat and me to her house, showed us around, and said, "I'd like you to take anything and everything you like of my furniture. It's yours." She meant it. She wouldn't have minded if we had backed up a truck and cleaned her out. She told us that. We wound up taking one mahogany table as a keepsake.

It strikes me that we lock ourselves into a room of unreasonableness sometimes. It may be an addiction, a sin, an ungodly lifestyle. It violates God's reasonable order. It becomes a very defensive way of living. We have to keep slamming the door on God and others to maintain it, making up excuses as we curl into a dark corner with our sin.

When Isaiah knocks on the door, he has something from God to offer us.

A Future Redeemer

Paralyzed by their fears of the Assyrian army, the Israelites, Isaiah announces, should instead be appalled by their sin. They are a people walking in darkness. Fortunately Isaiah offers more than a reprimand. He tells the people to hope and keep watch: a Redeemer is coming.

The people heard, around the rim of their borders, the hoofbeats of the terrible Assyrian army preparing to march. But like drumbeats of a distant victory parade, Isaiah heard the Redeemer coming.

And when he comes, what will he do?

Isaiah makes it clear that the Redeemer will cleanse people from sin. "Though your sins are like scarlet, they shall be as white as snow" (Isaiah 1:18). When people are reasonable and repentant about their sin, the Redeemer will cleanse them from it. Isaiah echoes this great theme of forgiveness throughout his book. He pounds it into the ears of a people gone deaf with their own babbling. In Isaiah 43:25 the prophet proclaims a message direct from God: "I, even I, am he who blots out your transgressions, for my own sake, and remembers your sins no more."

With his keenly prophetic eye fixed centuries in the future, Isaiah is absolutely clear about how this will occur. In Isaiah 9 we are told that a son will be given. Indeed, he will be a great counselor, a prince of peace. But the full wonder of his counsel isn't revealed until Isaiah 53. By his wounds people can be healed. He will be oppressed and afflicted and led like a lamb to the slaughter. He will "pour out his life unto death" and bear "the sin of many."

Moreover, this Redeemer will bring peace. How the people, living in the darkness of constant threat, longed for a glimpse of peace. Our God, Isaiah boldly announces at the outset, is a peace bringer: "They will beat their swords into plowshares and their spears into pruning hooks" (Isaiah 2:4). And however fierce the foreign armies appear, they are nothing, Isaiah says, before the absolute power of God. To these nations Isaiah almost mockingly charges: "Devise your strategy, but it will be thwarted; propose your plan, but it will not stand, for God is with us" (8:10). Our God is a Lord of triumph—the Old Testament testifies repeatedly to God's direct intervention in human affairs to protect his people in peace.

But peace of a political sort is not the most significant kind of peace. Isaiah is well aware of that. Then, as now, people could live in peaceable external circumstances while their hearts and minds raged with internal conflict. For these people also Isaiah has a word, for God is not just a God of lordly dominion over political events; he is also the loving Lord who bends the hearts of his people and speaks his powerful peace into them. Isaiah 25 gives a glorious glimpse of how the Redeemer will enact this. It is more than a careless promise; it is a pledge of a reality to come. On this mountain, Isaiah says, "The Sovereign Lord will wipe away the tears from all faces; he will remove the disgrace of his people from all the earth" (v. 8).

That inner peace is what the people long for; it is enacted by Jesus on "this mountain" of Calvary.

Isaiah 26 defines the nature of that peace more closely. Speaking of God, Isaiah says: "You will keep in perfect peace him whose mind is steadfast, because he trusts in you. Trust in the LORD forever, for the LORD, the LORD is the Rock eternal" (vv. 3-4). Isaiah's use of the phrase "perfect peace" is interesting, for it may be translated from the Hebrew as "peace times peace," like a mathematical equation. It is peace beyond our comprehension, beyond our ability to measure. It is the inner peace that sustains us, miraculously, even in the raging storm. It is very much like Jesus on the turbulent sea of Galilee, speaking peace to the billows about him. So too his peace infiltrates our disquieted and often storm-tossed hearts.

But what makes all this possible? What turns it from a divine promise into a pledge of historical reality? What puts a face, flesh and bone, on the promises?

At the dramatic climax of his vision, Isaiah tells us precisely for whom we keep watch. After the soul-stirring chapters of 40—50, full of verses that ring like trumpet peals in our ears, Isaiah makes a transition to his vision of the Redeemer, and then in chapter 53 defines the heart of his message. Not just peace, not just victory, but *Someone* will come as peace bringer. And he will do it in the most unexpected way. There will be no physical lordliness about him, no huge earthly power—in fact, he will be a man of sorrows, someone we would turn our faces from.

It is what he is and what he does that's important. Not what he looks like.

The Redeemer will take our sorrows on himself. Our peace will be enacted through his suffering. Now we begin to understand peace a little better. It isn't just the temporary alleviation of stress or disquiet; rather, it is a peace that lasts forever. "Perfect peace" is the peace that prevails into all eternity.

Isaiah tells the rest of the story of what he will do: "He was wounded for our transgressions, he was bruised for our iniquities: the chastisement of our peace was upon him; and with his stripes we are healed" (53:5 KJV).

From his side of the crucifixion, Isaiah peers down the narrowing scope of years and sees a horror befalling the Redeemer that nonetheless enacts the redemption. It baffles the mind. Yet he rejoices in it, for by it is established our *perfect* peace.

From our side of the crucifixion, we who are keeping watch for the Redeemer find the vision no less disturbing. In fact, those words— "with his stripes we are healed"—slip into the heart like cold fingers and squeeze.

The words are clothed in mysteries, beset by too many paradoxes for the human mind to contain comfortably. In the very pain arises healing? From the act of cruelty springs kindness? In the suffering comes forth peace? These were stripes that maimed and hurt. They rose and fell and snapped at the flesh, cutting deep, ragged gouges. They were the stripes of torture—the sheer, unadulterated agony of dying.

There was no healing for the sufferer, yet the stripes did heal. By his dying we live. In the chastisement lies our peace.

In this world brutality against human flesh and human spirit destroys and maims for a lifetime. The scars cannot be effaced by any earthly power. We cannot escape suffering, no matter how desperately we try. The stripes continue to be laid—not always visibly; sometimes like raw, bleeding wounds on the heart itself.

The stripes drive us running away in full, panicked flight from the pain. We run looking for peace, looking for a safe place.

Jesus found no safe place on that bleak morning. There is the mystery of healing prophesied by Isaiah: a grace beyond our comprehension that meets horrors we don't understand. Meets the pain, takes it and provides heart-healing for it. With his stripes, we find God's perfect peace. When the whip cracked and snapped across Jesus' back, like a scythe ripping the tender flesh, there was no hiding place. Unless, as an old song has it, we hide him in our hearts. Surely we do so, but if we only hide him there it is insufficient. If Jesus' suffering was the enactment of grace for us, then it seems reasonable, truly reasonable, that we accept the grace with one desire: to bring it to those still suffering in these troubled times.

By grace we give grace; by Jesus' perfect peace we become peace bringers.

For Further Study

Read Isaiah 60

1. Isaiah lived more than seven hundred years before Jesus was born. How would Isaiah 60 sound if it were spoken in Bethlehem at Jesus' birth, or even today as we look back at that birth?

2. How does that sense of historical unity (2,750 years) affect our understanding of peace as it is discussed in this chapter?

3. We can confirm our peace if we can identify those things that threaten it. Pause for a moment and create a list of such things in your mind. Which of them do you have control over? Those you can't control you have to turn over to God. For those within your control you need to ask God's direction, grace and help to resolve.

4. What is our greatest peace in God? What is it that Isaiah calls "perfect peace"?

5. Before we can find the "perfect peace," Isaiah calls us to a "reasonable" accounting for our sins. How do the two necessarily work together? How are they, in fact, inseparable?

Prayer

There are times, Lord, when it is both good and necessary to confess, to set the record straight and try to set things anew. I confess all things and anything that stands between me and you. To my embarrassment and shame I name them. I ask for and thank you for your forgiveness. I thank you that you are a God who loves me so much that you are jealous for my love. Therein lies my perfect peace, and for that I love you, Lord.

4

How Then Shall We Live?
AMOS

*I*T SEEMS THAT MANY OF THE PROPHETS' LIVES WERE AN ENIGMA. SUDdenly, at one place and time in history, they step out of the shadows and prophesy with a piercing clarity.

What do we really know about them? They didn't grow up in royal households, where careful records might be kept. Few of them held important positions in the political arena. Many practiced the most common professions or traveled from place to place, sometimes oddly dressed, like Isaiah and John the Baptist. About some of them we know next to nothing. Isaiah's wife was a prophetess. We don't even know her name. Huldah was a prophetess, the wife of a man named Shallum, living in the city of Jerusalem during the reign of Josiah. But her work is represented by only a few verses in 2 Kings 22 where she confirms the high priest's discovery of the Book of the Law.

Yet each of the prophets, regardless of his or her obscurity, was touched powerfully by God's Spirit to be spokespersons to the age and for the future. Their central message unifies them in a common cause: keep watch. Don't become lost as a part of this world; live for the world to come under the reign of the Anointed One.

But how do we live in *this* world while keeping watch? That is the question central to Amos's prophecy.

Amos was a near contemporary of Isaiah, living and prophesying a few years before Isaiah in the same southern kingdom of Judah. Amos's hometown of Tekoa lay just a few miles down the road from Bethlehem. It was a region used primarily for sheepherding, and this was Amos's profession. One recalls the angel's appearance to shepherds in the fields near Bethlehem at the nativity. What a splendid tie to Amos, who lived and worked in those same fields nearly eight hundred years before.

Even though he lived slightly before Isaiah, the tensions Amos felt were much the same. It was a land under siege of darkness, with threats to the kingdom arrayed externally and internally. While Isaiah spoke words of peace and promise to a people walking in darkness, Amos spoke of how we are to live until the promise is fulfilled and the light shines. Thus Amos's message has profound implications for God's people today also. For if the light has appeared in Christ Jesus, all the more emphatic are the directions for Christlike living. It would be fair and accurate to say that all of Amos's prophetic teachings are endorsed by Jesus himself. They are, in fact, timeless teachings. They grow directly out of the spirit of the Mosaic law and the Ten Commandments; they are encoded on our hearts by Jesus' new commandment to love one another.

When Jesus said in Matthew 5:17, "Do not think that I have come to abolish the Law or the Prophets; I have not come to abolish them but to fulfill them," our ears should be tuned carefully to the words of Amos. On this side of the Incarnation, with Jesus' ringing endorsement, we have all the more reason to pay close attention to the question of how we shall live as God's redeemed people. While Amos kept watch for a Redeemer, and told his people how to live while keeping watch, we too keep watch for the full coming of the Redeemer's kingdom and need to know how to live as Christ's people as we keep watch. The lessons of Amos are a road map for Christian living, directing us in the ways of justice, righteousness and truth.

The book of Amos opens with dire judgments on Israel's neighbors, but even here the central message to God's people appears. The sins of these nations include "disregarding the treaty of brotherhood" and "stifling all compassion." Some fundamental human decency and justice are abrogated in favor of the power of selfhood. And, as his charges shift from pagan nations to Judah and Israel, the charges themselves remain fundamentally the same, "They sell the righteous for silver, and the needy for a pair of sandals" (2:6). In matters of human justice and spiritual righteousness, God's chosen people are indistinguishable from pagan nations. Here is the crime: a forfeiture of lovingkindness to fellow humanity for self-interested gain. We have placed ourselves on the throne of God. It is a sin as old as Eden.

Amos's assumption is that God has established a just order for society. Justice is constituted of a vertical relationship of worthy, heartfelt worship of God, and then is manifested in a horizontal relationship of loving care for fellow humanity. Justice is always, then, a twofold act. The lack of just dealings with fellow humanity indicates a rottenness at the spiritual core of God's people. The action of justice has withered like fruit on a stricken vine. There must be pruning and care to restore spiritual vitality.

From such a premise Amos levels specific charges against the people. Here's the wrong; this must be pruned away and corrected. And, properly, he begins with the vertical relationship. Our dealings with others are always a manifestation of our dealings with God.

I was fishing at a pond back in the hills of Appalachia one summer evening when a farmer tramped in from his field and stopped to talk with me. He wanted to talk about religious matters, but there was a bitterness in his voice that made me uneasy. As he left he said, "Show me how much you love others, and I'll show you how much you love God." It was one of those comments that lingers a long time in the mind before you simply acknowledge that it's the truth.

Misdealing with others breaks God's just order, his shalom, for society. Correction begins with restoration of a right relationship with

God. To turn God's people back to worthy worship, Amos identifies three sicknesses in their devotional lives.

Three Spiritual Illnesses

First among these sicknesses, Amos charges, is that the people have permitted their relationship with God to degenerate to mere *ritualistic worship*. The people do worship, but out of a habit they scarcely understand. Nor do they much care to understand. They sit in the pews, in modern terms, and overhear the religious noises while their minds wander over investments, projects or the afternoon activities. They are a people asleep in the Lord's house, taking a spiritual nap at the throne of Almighty God.

Such a ritualistic worship, Amos proclaims, God hates. It is a worship of mere presence, not of the heart. Thus he speaks for the Lord: "I hate, I despise your religious feasts; I cannot stand your assemblies. Even though you bring me burnt offerings and grain offerings, I will not accept them. Though you bring choice fellowship offerings, I will have no regard for them" (5:21-22). Properly understood—that is, by the individual heart—these are terrifying words. To be told that God will have "no regard" for our offerings, that he "cannot stand" our religious assemblies, cuts our pretenses of spiritual commitment off at the knees. Rightly so, for it leaves us on our knees begging forgiveness.

In this same passage Amos makes a direct connection between our worship and our engagement of social justice. The clear and irreducible point is that if we are rendering worthy worship to God, we will bring that worship to action in social justice. Conversely, our failure to enact social justice mirrors the hollowness of our spirituality: "Away with the noise of your songs! I will not listen to the music of your harps. But let justice roll on like a river, righteousness like a never-failing stream!" (5:23-24). The two, spirituality and social justice, are so powerfully intertwined that they necessarily affect each other positively or negatively.

If we were to be given a test to chart the degree of our spirituality and closeness to God, here is a beginning point. Is our faith enacted in deeds? Do our deeds incarnate our faith? James makes this point perfectly clear in his epistle: "As the body without the spirit is dead, so faith without deeds is dead" (2:26). Theologian Carl Henry put it another way in *A Plea for Evangelical Demonstration* (Baker, 1971): "The Bible calls for personal holiness and for sweeping societal changes; it refuses to substitute private religion for social responsibility or social engagement for personal commitment to God" (p. 107).

If Amos's first charge against God's people is a mere ritualism in worship and a consequent ignoring of social justice, his second charge may be worded simply as a *spiritual laziness.* Chapter 6 begins with a condemnation of complacency, and he spares no words in his disparagement of the people. With a scarcely veiled satire, he accuses them of pretending to be king David—their spiritual forefather: "You strum away on your harps like David and improvise on musical instruments. You drink wine by the bowlful and use the finest lotion, but you do not grieve over the ruin of Joseph" (6:5-6). This is sharply barbed ridicule; perhaps it was necessary to get people's attention.

One wonders what Amos would say if he lifted the cover off our spiritual lives today, and whether he would find us complacently asleep in the Lord or keeping watch for opportunities to serve him. The danger of complacency is that it leads directly to Amos's third charge: *spiritual cowardice.*

The steps are clear. When religion devolves to ritual, and when people become complacent in that ritual itself, then it almost naturally follows in this downward spiral that the people become fearful of speaking God's name altogether. We draw protective little blankets around ourselves. They protect us from the encroachment of others; they prevent us from reaching out to others. As the blankets thicken, they even prevent us from hearing the voice of God.

As a college teacher, I often hear my students wondering what profession God has in store for them. When they tell me this, I carefully explain that "God has a calling in mind for you, but it is you whom he is calling." The first thing is to have a personal relationship with the Lord and to listen for his leading. Sometimes we listen with ears turned stone deaf by the world's cacophony.

Amos's portrait is even more desperate. Foreseeing disaster for God's people, Amos pictures them hiding—and dying—in their houses of complacency. And when someone asks, "Is anyone with you," the frightened voice answers, "No . . . Hush! We must not mention the name of the LORD" (6:10). They are people isolated in abject fear.

But Amos provided his own example of what is right in this matter of speaking the name of the Lord. Amaziah, the priest of Bethel, grew disturbed with Amos's teachings. Little wonder, with Amos's barbs against organized religion of his day. To stifle the truth-sayer, Amaziah sent a message to King Jeroboam saying, "The land cannot bear all [Amos's] words" (7:10). They were too rude, too threatening and entirely too accurate.

Amos himself does not threaten. He explains how God took him away from his own complacent life as a shepherd, and how God gave him a message. Amos says he cannot stop speaking out, no matter what Amaziah or the king says. His task is to speak in the name of the Lord.

But why? Why couldn't Amos just be quiet and go away? Herd your sheep, Amos. That's the safe course.

He couldn't because he was faithfully keeping watch. Amos details the end, the purpose, of his vision. The closing words foretell both Jesus' crucifixion and the end times before Jesus returns.

Once again denouncing the greedy who trample on the poor on their headlong rush to wealth, Amos plunges us headlong into the advent of the Messiah. Specifically, Amos tells us to look for a day when God will "make the sun go down at noon and darken the earth in broad daylight" (8:9). While this statement bears general apocalyptic importance, it was specifically fulfilled at the crucifixion, when the sun did in fact disappear behind a dark sky at noon. Then the people who rejoiced in their rituals, the passage continues, will be thrust into mourning. But for whom? Not just for themselves but "mourning for an only son"—the only Son of God, the Messiah.

This is the one for whom we keep watch, and surely Jesus cuts a line among humanity—those who tremble fearfully at his presence or those who rejoice in his mercy. It is precisely because of that vision that Amos holds out the hope of mercy in the final chapter of his book. When God's people return to him in righteous worship and just living, he is a God of generous mercy.

Becoming Spiritually Well

Amos's prophecy of the need for social justice and its integral relation with righteous worship should not be lost on us today. The fact is that many Christians are complacent in the pews; many separate their religious life from their professional life; many are too timid to speak the name of the Lord boldly at any given moment of their lives. Too often our allegiance lies in our culture rather than our God. In *New Strides of Faith* (Moody, 1972) Carl Henry observes, "Not only is this a go-go generation unsure where it is going, but ours is also a go-go-going culture that scarcely suspects it is about gone" (p. 9).

Amos's words seem to present a nearly imponderable challenge to us today. The world about us seems such a diseased and tormented thing that we want to shy away from it. It is so much easier to build walls to keep the world out. A glance at nearly any page of the newspaper brings scenes of human violation of other humans, often in such execrable ways and with such pointless abandon that we struggle to get them out of our minds. Go forth into *this* world to enact justice and righteousness? No thanks, Amos. It is too violent, too huge, and far too unwilling to listen. The world seems inured to justice by its long practice of criminality.

That's the way our thinking goes. We think in terms that are too large and are staggered into silence by the sheer proportions.

Amos, however, isn't suggesting that the Israelites run out and try to convert the Assyrian army. That may come, but only later. The first step is to get right with our individual selves. Justice and righteousness are first of all matters of the heart. "Hate evil, love good," Amos says. Get that straightened out first. Clean up your worship services; clean up your lives. You cannot enact justice and righteousness without holding them inwardly. But then, they will naturally flow outward—"like a never-failing stream." As actions of the heart, they will touch those closest to us first, touching our families, our friends, our coworkers.

God's message through Amos is not a polite request for social engagement, nor is it mere encouragement to "reach out and touch someone" in Jesus' name. It is a message of compelling urgency, one that ought to overflow in our own hearts. The need for social justice to roll down like a river is ever present in this world stricken by moral drought. The need for righteousness to flow like a never-ending stream is never more acute than at this present moment, when society wanders a spiritual wasteland. The brokenness of fallen humanity has diminished not at all since Amos's time. Sadly, not only is it in society about us, but appears in our own churches, in the same pew, sometimes in a seat at our own supper table.

We are seldom brave before our brokenness. Amos's words are no easy call to quick grace; they call us to enter into suffering in order to enact restoration of God's shalom in ruined lives.

It is a dangerous and demanding call, simply because people of our world—our families and churches also—so desperately need us to act as agents of restorative grace in their lives. In a world afflicted by evil that separates, by desire that twists, by indecency that destroys, we still hear Amos's message to seek common sense, to turn our desires toward God, to possess the bravery and decency both to embrace the cross and also to wrap our arms around our brothers and sisters in this human family, and to say with all our heart and soul and mind and strength, "I love you." How desperately we need those healing words and those healing hands around our own shoulders too. How necessary, on this side of the Incarnation, that we be Jesus to each other, loving, forgiving, unafraid to begin again.

This work requires a new heart. One cleansed of the corrosion of anger and bitterness. One liberated from greed that suborns others to our gain. One that admits our own deep guilt and shame and offers to Jesus our tears and begs him to turn them into joy.

Then, perhaps, the promise of Amos 9:14 will apply to us as well: "New wine will drip from the mountains and flow from all the hills." It will happen, because Jesus came as the new wine. And it will happen as the new wine of spiritual renewal flows through us in social justice and spiritual righteousness.

For Further Study

Read Amos 5

1. Waiting for our Savior is never a passive action. It seeks every opportunity to *find him at work* in our world and every opportunity for us to *work for him* in our world. What specific ways does Amos give for waiting, and how can we fulfill them?

2. In verse 18, why does Amos say, "Woe to you who desire the day of the Lord"? Doesn't that contradict everything we hope for and keep watch for? But in the larger context of the whole chapter, why does Amos say this?

3. What picture do we form from Amos's descriptions in this chapter? What specific verses identify certain qualities of the Lord?

4. What is the major theme of this chapter? Is it God's mercy to us? Our mercy to others? What specific directions does it provide for our daily living?

5. "The world around us" starts inside our homes and extends from there. According to chapter four in this book, what is the first thing to get right before trying to change the world around us? Do you agree?

Prayer

Righteous—but merciful—Lord, who am I that I dare come before you? Yet through the storms of life you have always been there to carry me, so I come because I know you love me. I am your child. I am loved by the King of heaven and earth. Help me then also to show—to give and make real—your love and mercy to others. Amen.

5

A Man on His Knees
DANIEL

I REMEMBER THE DOWNSTAIRS AUDITORIUM IN THE OLD BRICK church on Fuller Avenue where we would gather for Sunday school. It seemed to me then that about a thousand kids packed the room and that the temperature kept going up. And as sweat popped out on our young faces, we bellowed songs until our lungs hurt—but the racket was all right because we were praising Jesus and the director kept encouraging us to give it all we had.

One song we belted out went something like, "Dare to be a Daniel, dare to stand alone ... ," and I remember thinking to myself as I sang, *No way! Not alone. No lions. No thanks.*

Daniel is the consummate biblical superhero—steadfast as granite in his convictions, bolder than the lions into whose den he was tossed, unswerving in his service to God. Other biblical heroes have their flaws that make them seem, when the whole story is told, mere mortals doing their best in a bewildering world. David was God's king, but also a hot-blooded sinner. Time and again he had to crawl back to God's throne, begging forgiveness. Moses, the appointed leader of

God's people, was God's mouthpiece, but he also had a temper so volcanic that he had to sit on a mountaintop and only look at the land others would enter. But Daniel? Bring a magnifying glass to his life and you still can't find a flaw. He is a hero, larger than life. He seems, to me, so far beyond me. Until I look more closely.

I still wouldn't much care to be Daniel, but in many ways I am called to be like him, as is any Christian. In a sense, Daniel *is* any Christian—a man on his knees seeking God's help. He was also, it becomes clear when one studies his topsy-turvy world of political tyrants, seeking the Messiah and his unending kingdom of justice and shalom.

Aside from his memorable adventures, however, few people today seem to know much about, or think about, or talk about Daniel. This is partly due to the nature of the book of Daniel. It skips around among historical events instead of presenting a clean chronology. It mingles literary forms freely, jumping from historical account to prophecies to visions. Parts read like a good short story; other parts like an obscure poem. Nonetheless, while there are a few barriers to understanding this remarkable person, it is worth the harder look for what he tells us—especially about prayer and keeping watch for the Messiah. With just a bit of historical reconstruction of the events in the book, these qualities become compellingly clear.

The overthrow of the kingdom, foreseen by Isaiah and Amos, had occurred. In the year 605 B.C., after defeating the Egyptians and conquering the Israelites, Nebuchadnezzar deported a number of young Jewish men from leading families to Babylon. Only the very best young men were taken: "young men without any physical defect, handsome, showing aptitude for every kind of learning, well informed, quick to understand, and qualified to serve in the king's palace" (Daniel 1:4). Basically, the king wanted the brightest and the best for his palace. Among the first group deported were Daniel and his three friends.

Such deportation is an old military ploy. Wars throughout history are marked by three options for the conqueror: annihilate the enemy, force slavery on the conquered, or permit them to live, work and make a profit to fill the coffers of the victor. Nebuchadnezzar was not necessarily being altruistic and merciful. The reputation of the Jews as fierce warriors and also as shrewd and prosperous businessmen was well known. Very likely Nebuchadnezzar brought this first group of Jews into exile to win them over to his side and also to benefit from their expertise in his court.

The only problem was that Nebuchadnezzar was the virtual deity in his kingdom. In fact, the significance of the name Nebuchadnezzar is often construed in two ways: "the treasure of Nebo" (Nebo was a Chaldean god, from which the king's name was derived), or "Nebo, the Prince of the gods." The two intertwine—of course the Prince of the gods should have a worthy treasure. And these young Jewish princes could help him obtain it. The only problem was that these young Jews, led by Daniel, worshiped their own God whom they refused to abandon, no matter what the price.

We tend to view these men as superheroes, but nothing could be farther from the truth. But they were, at least as Daniel's leadership indicates, men on their knees, awaiting the Lord's care in the time of trouble and the Lord's revelation for the time ahead. That twofold pattern may be clearly seen in Daniel's life as we consider his actions and his visions.

A Man of Action

I believe that it is wrong for any believer to say, "I surely don't have it as bad as Daniel. I'm not, after all, in the lion's den. Who am I to complain about my problems?"

Certainly the passages of Daniel's life were fraught with threat and disappointment. He was ripped from the friendly confines of his home at a young age and deported to a strange and distant land. There a fearfully powerful king started issuing commands that contravened everything Daniel believed in. The Babylonians did not observe any of the elaborate rules the Jews used to govern their diet. Yet Daniel and his friends had to challenge the king to remain faithful to God's rules of right and wrong. Over and over, it seemed, Daniel's fidelity to God's law raised the threat of death—in hideous ways.

We may do well to compare ourselves to Daniel's fierce loyalty; he is someone to emulate. The danger in such a comparison, however, is to think that because our problems seem relatively minor compared to his, they are of no consequence to God. Rather, the message of Daniel's life and his book seems to be that the Almighty Lord stands as ready to act with such a powerful authority in our lives as he did in Daniel's life.

Daniel's actions fall into two sorts: fidelity to God's law in the face of threats and execution of God's will as revealed to him in prayer.

Consider that first recorded test—the matter of diet. How easy it would be to rationalize the Jewish law away. I would have come up with a half dozen reasons real quick and then fallen to that good stuff the palace chefs were laying out. *I'm not in Judah,* I would have said to myself. *I'm in a strange land and have to adapt to survive. So what, after all, if the meat isn't prepared strictly in the ceremonial way? And I hate beans!* Then I would have added the reasoning that food taken physically into my body does not touch my mind and soul. *Very well, the body might be polluted a bit, but my devotion to the Lord is untouchable.*

That last bit of flawed logic becomes a handy excuse. The first time I heard something like it was when a platoon member in my army barracks started visiting prostitutes. It's just a bodily act, he argued—nothing spiritual. The trouble with that logic—not to mention sexually transmitted diseases—is that the division between the body and soul is a Greek concept. The heart of Christian thinking has a body-soul unity made in the image of God, redeemed by Christ and destined to be judged at the Second Coming.

Rationalization, by definition, offers a way out. It lets you do what you want to do rather than what you ought to do. The startling thing we recognize about Daniel is that he truly wanted to do what he ought to do. His desire and God's law were perfectly matched and bound in cords of mutual fidelity.

When Daniel and his friends decided not to partake of the palace food, then, they were not simply taking a stand *against* a kind of food; they were taking a stand *for* God's law. Essentially they were saying, "I will do this because this is what the Lord requires of me."

This matter of diet may seem like a little quarrel over vegetables or meat. More precisely, it was a line in the sand—"I will not cross over into your customs." And once that line was drawn, it served also as a declaration that this was important Daniel, and that he would not be shaken from his faith in God's law or power.

The actions of Daniel and his friends incarnate for us a vital spiritual psychology. Some Christians today, young or old, can spout scores of Bible verses like an overfull fountain. So too, there are some who have mastered doctrinal intricacies so arcane others of us hardly dare talk to them. However meritorious such achievements are, Daniel teaches us that our theology is a matter of the heart. It's a matter of where we stand and declare: This I believe; this I must do.

One of the books most formative in my own spiritual life, aside from Scripture, is St. John of the Cross's *Dark Night of the Soul.* In fact, when I was drafted during the Vietnam War, it was the only book beside a New Testament that I took with me. On the first day in our basic training company, a large garbage can was carried into the barracks while the sergeants confiscated "pornography, weapons and seditious literature." At one sergeant's order, *Dark Night* went into the garbage, right along with the glossy magazines and knives. Perhaps it was seditious. Here's what St. John has to say about matters of the heart: "True devotion must issue from the heart, and consists in the truth and substance alone of what is represented by spiritual things; all the rest is affection and attachment proceeding from imperfection." So the matter of diet, for Daniel and his friends, was more than an issue of vegetables or meat. It was a matter of devotion of the heart.

This early skirmish in fidelity, however, prepared Daniel for a more dramatic confrontation under the rule of Darius, Nebuchadnezzar's successor. The first thing Darius did was a bit of bureaucratic overhaul, appointing Daniel as one of three administrators over 120 regional satraps. Daniel was so distinguished in his task that Darius began to consider him as the ruler-in-chief over the whole enterprise. Fearful of this, others got together and hatched the plot to make official Darius's status as a god in the kingdom and to forbid worship of any other.

Daniel's reaction is fascinating. Without further ado he went home, got down on his knees and prayed. Which is exactly what the plotters wanted. In fact, "three times a day he got down on his knees and prayed, giving thanks to his God, just as he had done before" (Daniel 6:10). Daniel was destined for the lion's den.

So much for prayers, Daniel. See where they got you? A dinner out, with yourself as the main course.

Why are so many biblical heroes thrown into the depths? What remarkable courage. But those of us who have walked in the depths know the feeling. No words of Daniel are recorded here as he awaits the morning light. But I know what my words would have been—before the lions devoured me as surely they must: "Why me, Lord? It's not fair!"

King Darius also had a rough night. At the crack of dawn he was there at the pit, shouting for Daniel. And, remarkably, from out of the depths Daniel answered with praise for the king and testimony of God.

One wonders why Daniel was ever cast into the pit in the first place. If God was going to deliver him, why not do it *before* the depths? While we might cry out, "Unfair," we simply don't know God's scheme in leading us into the depths. It is clear that Daniel had to dwell there to experience God's deliverance. And it is also clear that the experience magnified God's name in the kingdom, for Darius ordered a decree for the whole kingdom to revere God Almighty. While it may have seemed prescriptive for the natives of the land, just one more decree from an addled king, it gave God's chosen people the freedom to worship him. At the end of the trial lay freedom and glorification. But for the trial, freedom and glorification would not have appeared.

Part of the lesson Daniel delivers to us who keep watch may go like this. Hold steadfast to fundamental beliefs, no matter how alien and foreboding the environment. When threat does appear, the first action is to get down on our knees and talk to God. And then understand that even though we may not discern God's will and plan, he has the power to lead us through trials to triumph. Daniel didn't know an angel was going to come and spend the night with him and the lions. But he did trust God whatever the circumstances. We may not see an angel at our side, but God has promised his presence with us.

A Man of Visions

If the book of Daniel is an important historical document, chronicling the life of the Israelites in exile, it is equally important as a book of prophecy. And in every prophecy, Daniel emphatically directs honor away from himself to God. When dreams trouble King Nebuchadnezzar's sleep, Daniel is brought to the court and asked if he can interpret dreams. Daniel explains that there simply is no wise man who can explain the dream, "but there is a God in heaven who reveals mysteries" (2:28).

A slight challenge arises here, because Daniel is also playing this divine game on the court of the Medes, the wise men of the empire. They are confident in their own wisdom, while Daniel looks beyond the human mind to the Creator of that mind.

The authority Daniel acquires by construing the king's dream is merely the entryway into more intense and increasingly complicated visions. The first prophecy to Nebuchadnezzar gave him comfort: "The God of heaven has given you dominion and power and might and glory" (2:37). But, oh, how transient is human glory. Robert Frost once wrote, "Nothing gold can stay." Especially not the golden crown of the earthly ruler. Kingdoms collapse; kings stagger into disrepute. A second time Nebuchadnezzar's dream opens on a vision acknowledging the fact that only the divine King who has ordained earthly kingdoms has absolute rule. Daniel declares, "Acknowledge that the Most High is sovereign over the kingdoms of men and gives them to anyone he wishes"

(4:25). For his defiance of this truth, Nebuchadnezzar stumbles down a precipice into insanity, finally groveling like a beast in the wilds. Not until he wakens from his madness does Nebuchadnezzar also acknowledge God as absolute ruler: "His dominion is an eternal dominion; his kingdom endures from generation to generation" (4:34).

The theme of the book of Daniel seems to switch directions at this point, from a testament of loyalty to increasingly complex visions of the Messiah and the final days. Actually, however, the first theme is a sort of prologue for the latter. Out of tested loyalty, Daniel is rewarded by glimpses into the future.

The first vision is recorded in chapter 7, like a page out of Daniel's diary. Through further chapters the vision accumulates detail about the advent of the Messiah 550 years in the future, and beyond that to the last days. Daniel sees the "Ancient of Days" take his seat among the other thrones. This is the King of kings, the absolute authority. To the Ancient of Days comes "one like a son of man" (7:13), the name Jesus often used for himself. Upon this Son of Man, the Ancient of Days bestows "authority, glory and sovereign power." But his rule is not some ephemeral, earthly kingdom; rather, "His dominion is an everlasting dominion that will not pass away, and his kingdom is one that will never be destroyed" (7:14).

But Daniel's visions are still not complete with the expectation of the Messiah. More complicated and mystical material appears. In fact, so troubled is Daniel that God's great messenger, the angel Gabriel, arrives to instruct him: "Daniel, I have now come to give you insight and understanding. As soon as you began to pray, an answer was given" (9:22-23).

This time, Gabriel explains, Daniel's prophetic vision opens on the destruction of the temple in Jerusalem, the arrival of the "Anointed One," or the Messiah, and the crucifixion: "After the sixty-two 'sevens,' the Anointed One will be cut off and will have nothing" (9:26). The Messiah will be cut off from his immediate, earthly ministry by his crucifixion. So all our hope is to end in death? So that evil can troop in and believers weep? The prophetic vision bears the rumble of warfare and the desolation of tears. It is a dire time ahead, enough to make the prophets quake. Is this a vision or a nightmare? Jerusalem will be in ruins; the Messiah will be cut off. If I were Daniel, I'd give in to despair.

In fact, for the first time, Daniel does. He fell down that gray abyss of hopelessness and mourning, huddled under the terror of the future. So he grieved for three weeks, until one morning he wandered down to the Tigris River and was stunned by the appearance of a huge, glowing angelic figure. He is terrifying—all Daniel's companions fled. But the angel's message was one of mercy: "Do not be afraid, O man highly esteemed. . . . Peace! Be strong now; be strong" (10:19).

Why should Daniel be strong, we might wonder? He has worn out his knees in prayer. He has witnessed the Lord's power, from opening the mysteries of visions to closing the mouths of lions. But when he looks fervently to the future, he sees only desolation. Indeed, and finally, Daniel sees only through human eyes. They are not the eyes of heaven. Warfare is rumbling through the heavens; the great angel Michael and others are wrestling our protection out of enemy-held territory. We are not now nor ever alone in keeping watch. If only Daniel had heavenly eyes, he would see other things also. He would see not just "the Anointed One cut off"; he would also see the risen Christ, standing triumphant over death itself, preparing a place for those who love him.

The life of Daniel, as well as this curiously compelling book, gives way at the end not to despair but to the hallelujah of a beatific vision. For these are the parting words of the angel: "Multitudes who sleep in the dust of the earth will awake: some to everlasting life, others to shame and everlasting contempt. Those who are wise will shine like the brightness of the heavens, and those who lead many to righteousness, like the stars forever and ever" (12:2-3).

Forever and ever we will shine, declares the angel. So it will be. Such is the hallelujah song of Daniel. We dare not, however, lose sight of the pleadings and prayers of Daniel before his voice found notes of joy. Time and again this life drove him to his knees. But he was in the right posture, for it would lead him to a time when he would stand among the stars.

For Further Study

Read Daniel 7:9-14

1. Chapter five claims that any Christian is called to be like Daniel. In what way is this so, especially today when we in the West don't have the immediate fear of religious repression that Daniel had?

2. What particular qualities did Daniel have that we should try to emulate (see Daniel 2:14; 2:27-28; 6:10)?

3. One might describe the book of Daniel as a book on the mysteries of God. Notice, for example, that in 2:28 Daniel says, "There is a God in heaven who reveals mysteries." But many of the mysteries remain unveiled. What examples of this occur in Daniel's own life?

4. When these "mysteries," or God's undisclosed will, appear in our lives, what are our responses? Does Daniel give us any guidelines here?

5. Daniel served in Babylon under three powerful rulers—Nebuchadnezzar, Belshazzar and Darius. Each challenged Daniel personally and spiritually beyond any one person's limits, yet Daniel endured. According to Daniel 7:9-14, what gave him a certain hope?

Prayer

Like Daniel, I want to be a person on my knees, my heart and hands open to you, Heavenly Father. When I am cast into confusing places where I don't understand why or what is happening to me, give me the strength you gave Daniel. Walk with me as you walked with him in the fire. I don't beg to know every mystery you keep; I pray only for your dear presence to be with me when I understand so little. Amen.

6

Courage in a
Time of Fear
ESTHER

*E*STHER IS, ACCORDING TO JEWISH LEGEND, ONE OF THE THREE most beautiful women who ever lived. Eve, the mother of all humankind, the woman shaped by the hand of God, is of course the paradigm of beauty. The second woman, Bathsheba, captured the heart of a king. She must have been remarkable to turn the head of David, God's chosen ruler, so that he gave in to his lust for a married woman.

Esther was indeed beautiful, winning one of the most important beauty pageants of ancient time. When she crossed the stage, Xerxes, supreme ruler of a vast kingdom, sat up and took notice. He stopped the procession of lovely ladies as abruptly as whiplash. This was the one—no doubt about it.

How terribly wrong it would be, though, for us to see Esther simply as a heart-stoppingly beautiful woman who won the heart of some tyrant about 460 years before Christ. She was not only lovely; she also had a heart as bold and brave as an eagle in flight.

Let me quickly add that I have nothing against beautiful people. In fact, I married one, and she has only grown more beautiful during the thirty years of our marriage. But I quickly and freely admit that I am not as attractive. Nor am I particularly envious of beautiful people, because sometimes others see them only as beautiful *objects*—like a delicate Tiffany lamp, something to gawk at. Beauty, as well as disfigurement or impairment, can in fact be a kind of shield preventing others from seeing the real person inside.

Certainly Xerxes made this mistake at first, as he saw Esther paraded across the room in a train of female beauties. He wanted a wife that was a beauty queen, a pageant winner complete with a free scholarship for a lifetime course in staying beautiful (all the free oils and potions you want) and a residence in the royal palace. Of course, there was a catch—the winner had to be ready at the king's behest any time. His former queen, Vashti, had been a woman who felt slighted, badly used. Her pride was offended by being treated like a pet beagle. Even though she was queen of the palace, Vashti was disposable—just a courtly functionary. And when she didn't function properly, she was stripped of her title and banned from the palace.

Xerxes initially saw Esther's beauty and beyond that, nothing. Esther, however, was a woman empowered by God. She would demonstrate a courage surpassing that of anyone in the kingdom. What Xerxes eventually found in Esther was a woman willing to give herself up, to sacrifice herself to liberate her people. She was willing to walk the road of trial, which could quite possibly end in death. Esther was, in fact, very much like another important person in biblical history. The superficial qualities are in stark opposition. While Esther was one of the most beautiful women that ever lived, this other person just wasn't much to look at. He "had no beauty or majesty to attract us to him, nothing in his appearance that we should desire him." He was "like one from whom men hide their faces" (Isaiah 53:2-3). Uniting these two persons, so different in appearance and separated by 460 years of history, were their hearts. Both were ready to lay down their lives for those whom they loved.

Esther's Story

Esther's story occurs during the exile of the Jews, some years after Daniel's time in Babylon. Xerxes had succeeded his father Darius, and ruled from 486 to 465 B.C. It is a very unusual passage in Jewish history. While Daniel boldly spoke about his God and the coming Messiah, the pagan rituals now had clamped down once again with a suddenness and thoroughness comparable to the restrictive persecution of Stalin's communism in the Soviet Union. It was a dangerous thing to profess faith in God during Esther's time. Religion had gone underground among the Jews. This persecutorial climate undoubtedly accounts for the fact that this is the only book in the Bible that does not mention God's name. But he is very much there, appearing in symbols and actions that the exiled Jews would readily understand. But so too is the Messiah there in actions and symbols that we can understand and take courage from.

The story unfolds with Xerxes giving a huge party for his royal friends, lasting 180 days, in celebration of his conquests. Simultaneously, Queen Vashti is throwing a party for the royal women. Toward the end of these lengthy revelries, the king drunkenly sends for Vashti to parade her beauty before his men. He expects her to obey quickly, of course, because not only is the dominant authority of men customary, but Xerxes is the *sole* authority in the land. When Vashti refuses him, Xerxes deposes Vashti. There is not much discussion about it, and there does not have to be. Xerxes just calls it as he sees it.

But kingship can be a lonely business. In time, Xerxes feels the need for a new queen. Thus the beauty pageant. After a year of preparation, the candidates file past, and Esther wins hands down.

But there's a rat in the palace. His name is Haman, and his goal is to destroy the Jews entirely. He hates them bitterly. His narrow little soul is on fire with a longing for destruction. As one of the leading nobles in the kingdom, Haman starts his plot of extermination by requiring all the Jews to bow down before *him.*

In the minds of some of those Jews, despite years in exile, there live echoes of the old Jewish Holy Books. Words like these still spoke to them: "Hear, O Israel: The LORD our God, the LORD is one. Love the LORD your God with all your heart and with all your soul and with all your strength" (Deuteronomy 6:5). Or perhaps these words: "You shall have no other gods before me. . . . You shall not bow down to them or worship them" (Deuteronomy 5:7-9). One such Jew was Esther's uncle, Mordecai. When he refused to bow down before Haman, the jealous tyrant flew into a fit of rage, and "looked for a way to destroy all Mordecai's people, the Jews, throughout the whole kingdom of Xerxes" (Esther 3:6).

Here's what this schemer, this vengeful little man, does. He dupes the king. Xerxes' treasury was reaching a low point after fighting the costly Greek wars and then throwing a six-month victory party. Haman solicits the king's permission to kill and plunder the Jews and to pay a certain amount of his profit into the king's treasury. It's an offer Xerxes can't refuse.

Hearing the news, Mordecai undertakes the Jewish ritual of mourning, in sackcloth and ashes. He becomes an emissary for his people but he needs someone else to enact their liberation. Someone close to the king. There is no other Jew, anywhere, who even has access to the king except his niece, Esther. His words to Esther are fearfully direct: "Do not think because you are in the king's house you alone of all the Jews will escape. For if you remain silent at this time, relief and deliverance for the Jews will arise from another place, but you and your father's family will perish. And who knows but that you have come to royal position for such a time as this" (Esther 4:13-14).

Then this bold, beautiful woman acts, and it is no simple act. For violating the king's request, Vashti was deposed. What Esther risks is infinitely more complicated; she braves death itself to rescue her people. She must enter the throne room of the king, a place no woman was permitted to go and no man was allowed to go unbidden. Esther violates all the rules. She stands in the court waiting Xerxes' recognition—or fury. It is difficult to imagine her emotions at this most precarious point in her young life. Her body must have rocked with tremors of anxiety as she waited one step away from life or death. Xerxes notices her, frozen in the doorway. Then, miraculously, he points his golden scepter at this rule-violator and bids her enter and speak.

The rest of the story contains a series of dramatic ironies, reversals and plot twists that have long made this book one of the most exciting and engaging in the Bible. The vainglorious villain Haman is humbled and hung on the gallows he built for Mordecai. Mordecai is elevated to a high position in the kingdom. Esther further intercedes for her people, ensuring their safety, and the Jewish feast day of Purim, a time of festivity and celebration, is established.

The Rest of the Story
Is it just an exciting story, celebrating the beauty and bravery of a Jewish woman? The book of Esther is all of that, but it is much more. Here too we find one keeping watch, not in words and prophecy, but in her very person. Esther enacts an ideal pattern ultimately fulfilled in Jesus.

This pattern is not unusual in Scripture. For example, in the dramatic telling of Abraham's sacrifice of his son Isaac we have what biblical scholars call a *type.* God the Father's sacrifice of his son Jesus is then called the *antitype,* or the complete fulfillment of the type. What one individual enacts at one time is a partial fulfillment of what Jesus perfectly enacted in full and for all time.

The writers of the New Testament were keenly aware of this pattern of God acting through individuals at historical points to foreshadow the work of Christ. And they make specific connections for followers of Christ. To the Galatians Paul writes: "Consider Abraham: 'He believed God, and it was credited to him as righteousness.' Understand, then, that those who believe are children of Abraham. The Scripture foresaw that God would justify the Gentiles by faith" (Galatians 3:6-7). Later in that same chapter Paul makes the connection explicit: "If you belong to Christ, then you are Abraham's seed, and heirs according to the promise" (v. 29).

Abraham, however, is only one of many such types—those persons who by their actions and faith foreshadow the Christ. In the pattern also lies the beauty and unity of Scripture. Although written over the time of many hundreds of years, the Old and New Testaments are knit into a seamless whole of divine revelation. And in this pattern also falls the heroic young Jewish woman, Esther—a forerunner, a type, of Jesus himself.

It seems an odd claim, perhaps, because Esther is a book without specific mention of God. Yet certain actions recorded in the book are solidly rooted in the Jewish religious tradition. They were *actions* invoking God's presence rather than verbal declarations testifying to it. When Mordecai shows his lamentation by wearing sackcloth and ashes, he is enacting a religious ritual. When Esther asks Mordecai to gather the Jews in Susa together to fast for three days, prayer would certainly be a part of the tradition. And, one suspects, it would be prayer about Esther's meeting with Xerxes.

The prayer does not go unheard; there is divine intervention. Chapter 6 recounts how Xerxes could not sleep one night, so he orders the chroniclers of his reign to be brought in. It was like someone getting up to watch late-night television today. It almost immediately puts one to sleep. But as Xerxes listens, a curious thing happens—something that startles him wide awake. He is directed by God to the story of Mordecai, who turned in two traitors to the court some years before. This is unfinished business; Mordecai deserves an honor. It sets up the triumph of Mordecai over Haman, as Xerxes not only honors Mordecai but also desig-nates Haman as the one to carry it out.

The pleading intercessions of God's people in Babylon bear striking similarities to our own lives. We often may not see clearly God's will or way for our lives. We may see the suffering; we may see the threats to our peace; we may see our own need. Focused on those events that swirl like storm clouds, battering our hearts with bewilderment, we are unable to see God's hand working in authority to exercise his will no matter how hard Satan buffets and tosses our lives. Sometimes it isn't for many years that we can say, "Oh, yes. I see his plan now." Sometimes we won't be able to say that about our life until we arrive in eternity at Jesus' side. Then it won't matter.

The awesome power of the book of Esther lies in its testimony that God is there, working things out even when we cannot perceive him. Or even when events are so terrible that one dare not speak his name. On one of her moving albums Margaret Becker sings, "Say the name of Jesus, say the name that charms our fears. . . . Say the name that has heard our cry, seen our tears and wiped them dry." What she sings is true; the name alone is powerful: "For there is no other name under heaven given to men by which we must be saved" (Acts 4:12). But there are times—during the Vietnam War or during the Stalin years—when for captives to speak that name bears the consequence of death. Such a time it was for Esther. So too we understand the bravery of her heart and the beauty of her spirit; they arose from her loyalty to God.

While the book is important to us for its testimony to God's presence, it is also important to us for the human representation of Christlikeness in Esther herself. Consider the specifics of the story in this light.

When Mordecai adopted the posture of lamentation, with his clothes torn and replaced with sackcloth and ashes, he did so not for himself, but for his people. He was an intercessor for a people condemned by Haman's greed. Since the Jews were already a people in exile, a people living under constant threat, Haman's plan was a very real and pertinent threat; lives were at stake. So Mordecai appealed to Esther, the only one on the earth who might save them.

For Esther to act on Mordecai's request and for her people was nothing to be taken lightly. The risk was real and immediate and she knew it: "For any man or woman who approaches the king in the inner court without being summoned the king has but one law: that he be put to death" (4:11). The exception was for the king to extend the golden scepter, but Esther frankly was not hopeful. Thirty days had passed since the king last summoned her. Even though a queen, she was an outsider to the court. And Xerxes was a moody, tyrannical man, capable of volcanic fits of temper. Death was a very immediate likelihood.

Nonetheless, to save her people Esther went ahead with her task. She alone could intercede.

Esther went alone on earth, but God did not desert her. This God turned Xerxes' thoughts to troubled reflections during the night, and turned the chronicle to Mordecai's deeds. This same God had turned Xerxes' eyes to Esther above all the women of the kingdom. This God walked with Esther every step. And he will do the same for us.

The very reason we grasp that confidence, sometimes with trembling heart and fumbling hands, is that God walked his own lonely path. Jesus stood alone—but for his people—precisely as Esther did. Esther did not know the outcome of her lonely walk; it might be life or death. Jesus knew absolutely the outcome of his; it was death that gives eternal life.

But there is one final lesson here for those of us who keep watch. That work of Esther, like that of Jesus, ends in joy. Esther's ordeal ended in celebration and festivity: "For the Jews it was a time of happiness and joy, gladness and honor" (8:16). The people feasted and celebrated throughout the kingdom. So too, for the people of Jesus, comes the expectation of joy at the end of trials: "He will wipe every tear from their eyes. There will be no more death or mourning or crying or pain" (Revelation 21:4).

The lesson of Esther is not that we will escape every suffering or trial in our lives by a twist of divine intervention. Rather, it is that because Jesus endured the ultimate trial for us, we look forward to deliverance into joy.

For Further Study

Read Esther 4

This selection from Esther gives us several very important clues about the book:

The Jews are in exile under a king who was not favorably disposed toward

Jews or their God. Why? Because Xerxes saw himself as the absolute authority in the land. He didn't want that threatened.

Nonetheless, the Jews had prospered in exile. God had watched over them. Because of their success, Haman had talked Xerxes into kingdomwide genocide of the Jews to seize their goods.

The acts of fasting and praying would clearly be religious practices to God, even if God isn't mentioned.

And everything depends on Esther.

1. Esther acquires her position through her beauty—or was it God's design? So often we too, like Xerxes, look on the surface and fail to see the heart. Compare Esther's selection with King David's in 1 Samuel 16:7. See also Luke 16:14-15.

2. In Esther 4:13-14 Mordecai gives Esther a very unusual challenge. He believes that deliverance will come, but he also believes God has a plan *now* for Esther to act. How can we know God's plan for our actions? Is it sometimes the case, as with Esther, that we can't know *unless* we act?

3. In what ways does Esther resemble Jesus?

4. What are the primary lessons of the book of Esther?

Prayer

Dear Lord, I know that like Esther I can't escape trial and suffering. Only be with me, Lord. And when I'm called to act, help me choose wisely and act in faith. I thank you that in such moments I can know the power of the risen Christ acting in me. Amen.

7

Pondering
the Impossible
MARY

*S*EVERAL YEARS AGO, WHILE VISITING WASHINGTON, D.C., I
drove with my family to the national shrine for the Virgin Mary
just north of the city. The cathedral was an awe-inspiring structure, huge and soaring in the pattern of certain foreign cathedrals
I have seen. Detailed artwork covered the stone interior. On the
lower level a large space had been set aside to sell Mary memora-
bilia—everything from rosary beads to porcelain roses, from hand-
kerchiefs to praying hands, from tea cups to anointing oil.

I thought of Mary in the stable, giving birth, taking her infant,
wrapping him in some cloths, and laying him in the manger. I know
this latter Mary, not the product of commercialism, but the country
maid, making the best of a difficult task because of her powerful heart.

I wonder what Mary felt. She had not studied a stitch of theology
in the big city. She couldn't make it past the public altar of the temple.
The only eschatology she knew was the passing of seasons above the
hill-rolling farms near Nazareth. No scholar was Mary; hers was a
simple faith. She walked paths of innocence.

Listen. It is a faith beyond value. The kind of faith I cry out for. Oh, to be like Mary, child of a simple faith. For to such belongs the kingdom of heaven. And she, of all people, carried the King of heaven within her. Mary is a miracle of faith to sing about. She is the lyrical energy of our hallelujahs. We rejoice because of Mary.

While a young woman, probably only a child of fourteen, she was engaged to and eventually wed Joseph, who was in the lineage of David. They were relatively poor. And they started off married life with what most consider a drawback—a premarital pregnancy. But this wasn't the curse that some people thought it was. Mary held that secret in her heart.

She had been visited by an angel, and not just any angel. This was Gabriel, the messenger from the throne of God. This same angel appeared at least twice to Daniel in order, as he said, "to give [him] insight and understanding" (Daniel 9:22). Gabriel sketched a panorama of human history for Daniel, climaxing in the reign of Christ. How fitting that it was Gabriel who delivered the glad news to Mary. Gabriel himself had been keeping watch. I bet he was just bursting with the news: The Messiah will be born! Here! Now!

This country girl was blessed with faith and boldness. When Gabriel first greeted her, Mary was greatly troubled. But when he reassured her and delivered the message of her impending pregnancy, she simply asked, "How will this be since I am a virgin?" (Luke 1:34). It's a practical question. And with an uncommon sense of composure, she committed herself fully to the course God had chosen, "I am the Lord's servant. . . . May it be to me as you have said." That's the whole of it. No bargaining, no pressing for details, no discussion. Surely Mary is one of the great heroes of faith.

Apparently trusting God with her plight as an unwed parent, she wrote a song to express her joy. A gifted young poet, she captured words like birds in flight and sent them soaring across the notes of the song:

My soul glorifies the Lord
and my spirit rejoices in God my Savior,

for he has been mindful
of the humble state of his servant. (Luke 1:46-48)
Her song rings with the vital power of a Davidic psalm.

Even though she possessed the gift that lets words sing, Mary was indeed a humble servant. Servanthood and humility are rare spiritual qualities at any point in history. Yet Mary dutifully undertook the long, dusty trip to Bethlehem, well into her pregnancy. She rode a donkey. She stayed at a no-stars stable. There she gave birth to the Messiah.

All these things we know for a fact about Mary. They are all recorded in the first two chapters of the Gospel of Luke. Knowledge is not always the same as understanding, however. What I fail to understand fully is the compassionate heart of this woman, her utter faithfulness, her fierce devotion.

It is that heart of Mary I want to know. That is where the mystery, but also her true nature, lies. I am helped by one verse—the mention of Mary's heart. This occurs just after the birth when the angels went leaping across heaven and performed a cosmic dance of joy before those bewildered shepherds. These country men outside Bethlehem decided to follow the angel's directions and leave their fields for the night. They found Mary's stable all right, and gabbled like a bunch of old country gossips telling everything the angels had said.

Mary knew, of course. Still, when she heard, she "treasured up all these things and pondered them in her heart" (Luke 2:19). I wonder what Mary pondered, what thoughts she mulled over. Because I want to move closer to that compassionate heart, ordained by God before time to be the mother of my Savior, I pause and, slowly now, ponder with Mary. Scripture keeps "these things" private, sealed up like a teenage girl's diary. I have to turn the pages with my own heart.

Well, what then might these things be that Mary pondered?

No doubt among them were the whirlwind events of the last few days, for there was much to remember. The long trip to Bethlehem, the hopeless housing situation, the birthing room of a stable. These things would roll through my heart and mind. Like a vacation trip gone bad, I would reflect and try to decide whether to laugh or cry.

But there were unusual things, departures from all normal experience that rip at the heart and leave one reeling and gasping for breath. They were enough to strike even the bravest soul dumb with wonder. This scene with the shepherds out in the fields, when the night heavens cracked open and the glory of the Lord shone around them. This was a thing to ponder, for it may have stirred recollections of other such celestial fireworks. Mary almost certainly had heard the account of Moses, walking up that mountain when the earth shook with thunder and lightning and when the glory of the Lord blazed like a devouring fire. When Moses beheld that glory, it so overwhelmed and enveloped him that when he walked down again the people were afraid of the afterglow on his face. He donned a veil to quiet the people's fears. Perhaps the shepherds also remembered that story—it was in the sacred texts their people had been raised on. If so, they knew what it signified: God come down among humans. And so the shepherds, having heard a choir of angels all adazzle with glory, trekked into Bethlehem. They had much to tell Joseph and Mary, their fellow country folk housed in a stable. Indeed that would be much to ponder for this maid, Mary.

What else could Mary find to ponder in her heart? Well, perhaps what she knew long before the angels and the shepherds made their official announcement.

Perhaps Mary pondered, first of all, a mystery so profound and personal that she knew not fully how to share it. It is a matter—this miracle—to savor for oneself, not to talk about. She is struck by the overwhelming force of mystery. This child is, at this moment, Mary's baby. Probably others held this baby; maybe the shepherds reached dirty fingers toward the newborn's hand, letting the infant's grip fasten for a moment. Maybe a nearby daddy tried an experienced hand at quieting the crying of this baby in the manger. But it was *Mary's* baby that they held. Did she become slightly nervous with the new mother's watchful care for her child? Surely she thought, *I have a baby boy! This is my glad news.*

Mary was a maid who had now given birth. Here was more for her to ponder. Although a virgin, a seed had been planted in her womb. Truly her ears received the angel's prophecy, and so too her heart was comforted by the Holy Spirit. But there is no need to think the baby's growth within Mary was anything but ordinary. This life inside her life grew. Mary was becoming a mother—an event so common yet each and every time so miraculous. And then, as weeks passed, as she felt the stirring, surely Mary marveled at this life within her life.

One has no need to make Mary superhuman, for that is not the pattern of God's work in human clay even from this first miraculous moment. Surely Mary felt disquiet. She knew the sickness and discomfort of pregnancy. It was the fullness of time, and the most unpropitious time—a time of travel and taxation and hurry. But it was, first of all for little mother Mary, this baby's time. Always it is so for the mother; so too for Mary.

She knew the nervous expectation as this small secret bulge enlarged, grew public, attracted notice. So Mary kept watch. Then the moment arrived that is only that motherly moment—in anguish and pain and in all the rude discomfort of her barnyard delivery room—yet that sweet motherly moment when the life within her life becomes its own life. A baby born.

Others held the baby now. But it would always be the mother's special moment. Her child lived, was held and was still her life, her child.

Out of the weariness of delivery, the recollection of the long expectation, the moment of birthing arrived and passed. A moment to remember in any mother's life: *I have given birth. This is my baby!* But Mary was a mother with more to consider, for to how many mothers had an angel appeared? And with what words! This life within her life was *God's* life! Surely a thing to ponder. God living within one, to be born by that one. This is what the angel called the baby: "The Son of God."

Back in Mary's lineage—way back, but she would have been mindful of him at this time of taxation and genealogy—was a poet. He wrote, "I am fearfully and wonderfully made." What a miracle and mystery this baby boy was she now held—the very God she worshiped. And what a fearful thing to name him: Son of God. She held in her arms the hope of all the world.

Oh, but Mary had much to think about that fearfully strange and wonderful night. For if this child was only her child, then there would be quiet in the stable—the solace of a husband, the pain after birth, the baby in need of a mother's breast. But Mary nursed the Son of God. And a jubilation of angels soared above the hillside. The word was out. Glory and exultation.

So the shepherds came, ragtag men of the hills, stinking of sheep and smoking fires, crowding into the crowded village, gawking at a manger, telling the mother what the angels had said. Great joy was on their faces: this child was also Savior—Christ the Lord. If her boy child was Savior to them, then he was to all humanity.

Breathlessly Mary looked down those years to all ages, remembering Gabriel's words of months past: "He will be great, and will be called the Son of the Most High." Not only son of Joseph and Mary, but Son of the Most High. "And of his kingdom there will be no end." How does one grasp how long forever is? How far does this child's kingdom extend? Perhaps she trembled at this and thought, *My child needs me as mother. His life depends on my life. But forever I and others will depend on him for life.*

Mary had these and many other things to think about as she went about taking care of her new child.

Some of Mary's mysteries we share and can ponder for ourselves. We see our own children or the children of others God has placed in our path. We try to grasp how each is at once a child of frail humans and a child of God.

Like Mary, we ponder also how the mystery of grace can penetrate the gritty reality of our lives in the person of Christ. She had such a compassionate heart, this woman ordained by God to mother God's Son. She reflects God's own compassion in allowing his Son to come to this earth, be born of a human and die for all humanity. Mary mothered God's Son, Jesus, and gave him up so that we can rise from the death of our sins and form a loving relationship with Christ here on earth and on through eternity.

Mary kept watch for a long time, convinced that God is faithful. Surely she kept expectant watch during the months of pregnancy. So too she must have kept a mother's eye on those who handled her new baby. But I'm thinking of another watch, on a day that held no joy for Mary. She watched across the darkened hilltop while lightning cut the blackness and illuminated her son dying on the cross. What did Mary ponder then?

Years earlier, before her baby was yet born, Mary had sung a song of rejoicing to the Lord. "From now on," she declared, "all generations will call me blessed" (Luke 1:48). But the blessedness, Mary proclaims, lies in the glory of the Lord revealed through her—and the hope within her. Here she accepts and affirms every word of Gabriel's prophecy. Now on this darkened, windswept hillside, this rocky knob of land outside of Jerusalem, Mary must have wept the tears of the hopeless as her son died. *Her* son.

Out of that darkness, however, grows the greatest lesson of Mary's watch keeping for us. Indeed, it would seem the end of all hope, if it were only her son that she grieved. But he was also the Son of God. The earth God had made could not contain him; no burial chamber could encase the Lord of life. If there was darkness on the windy heights of Golgotha, then dazzling radiance of life touched that resurrection morning when Jesus burst not just the bonds of stone and embalming linens but of death itself. The eternal significance of the radiance that morning made the dancing stars over the shepherds' heads mere child's play. They came to see a baby. The resurrection saw the Bright and Morning Star walk out of the darkness forever.

When the reports reached Mary—Jesus is alive!—what did she think then? I don't know, but I believe a deep solace of understanding flooded every nook and cranny of her soul. I think that—just maybe— she had nothing left to ponder. She knew. And as she heard the reports I like to think—but of course I don't know—that her lips parted in a quiet, secret smile. Maybe she whispered to herself, "Yes, I know."

So too, through Mary's pondering and her faithful watch keeping, do we know. Death is conquered. The darkness has been ruptured by light. There is a time coming for each of us when all we will know, all we will see, is the Daystar, who rules in the New Jerusalem where "the sound of weeping and of crying will be heard in it no more" (Isaiah 65:19).

As with Mary, it is a thing to ponder in our hearts.

For Further Study

Read Luke 2:1-20

1. Mary and Joseph were traveling from Nazareth to Bethlehem, the town where David was born (1 Samuel 17:12). The trip took approximately three days. Compare that to modern travel. How far in that time could you go by car? by foot?

2. What qualities come to your mind when you think of Mary? Would you include humility and grace?

3. In this chapter several things are suggested that Mary may have "pondered in her heart." Can you think of additional things? What might you ponder if you were Mary?

4. In Luke 1:29 we are told that upon hearing Gabriel's greeting, "Mary was greatly troubled at his words and wondered what kind of greeting this might be." What exactly troubles Mary? How does Gabriel respond?

5. Throughout the ages since Jesus' birth, people have elevated and celebrated Mary. But how is Mary just like any one of us? List her different emotions in the first two chapters of Luke. What do we find in her that resembles us?

Prayer

I am eternally grateful, Jesus, that you entered the world, born as human of human flesh to redeem the world. I also thank you for your mother, Mary. I thank you for her faithfulness and courage. I thank you for her belief during seemingly unbelievable events. I give thanks for her willingness to endure hardships. And with her, Jesus, I pray that my soul may magnify the Lord. Amen.

8

Holding the
Promise
SIMEON

*S*IMEON TOO IS ONE KEEPING WATCH, ONE OF THE VERY LAST, THE faithful one. Like a sentry on the watchtower, Simeon faithfully studied the land about him, looking for the Promised One. Days and years passed, and as they did, so too did the people before his watchtower. To be sure, many in those days claimed to be the promised one. There had always been; there always would be. How his heart must have been tempted by hope—surely this is the one!—only to sink, like feathers in the dust, to further waiting.

Slowly the years went by, and the years and the waiting were coming to an end. But like dust in the wind, the hopes scattered before his watching eyes.

Many people have known that torment of waiting—and that desert of disappointment. For some it has been a waiting through the long night hours, keeping watch for a son or daughter expected home long ago. The hours crawl like years then. The clock lies to the anxious eyes; surely it must be later than that. And then the clock flips its arrogant numbers in pure scorn; surely it can't be that late! And for some the waiting and watching never end. Though their children may eventually return to the house, they seem never to return to their spiritual home.

Or, for others, the waiting is the hard watch over a loved one's illness, wondering which way it will turn, and precisely when. We crave answers like basic nourishment. We cannot sustain our spirits without clear evidence. But finally there is only the helpless waiting to see what happens.

So too I have kept watch.

Ironically, it was on Mother's Day, 1994, that I first admitted my mother to the hospital via the emergency room. She was treated for a bladder infection, and a week later, after heavy dosages of antibiotics, was released. Over the course of spring and summer she was hospitalized four more times. For more tests at first. Then when the tumor was discovered, eating into the bladder wall, threading up through ureters to the kidney with its deadly malignancy, she was hospitalized for the bombardment of chemotherapy and radiation.

She changed during those months as she underwent her own waiting. She had lived eighty-one years of a flamboyant and energetic life, a fountain of laughter and a stream of grace. Certainly she was not without faults; who among us is? But she laid down her life for others, cutting a large swath through the days of her life that was marked everywhere by road signs of compassion, fiery energy and sacrifice. It is almost as if those road signs are propped there still: Here Went Carolyn Timmerman. She touched that many lives.

And when the sixth admittance to the hospital came, we came waiting not for recovery to this life but to life eternal. Even deep in a coma, she would still occasionally flinch a finger or let her lips tremble when I came and talked to her or kissed her goodnight. And so it went, long hours of waiting. We expected her to die long before she did. And when she did, it was 3:30 in the morning, the morning after my father's eighty-sixth birthday. Had she known? Had she too waited?

Keeping watch is so often an agony of uncertainty.

Yet isn't it also often an excitement of anticipation? Other images crowd the mind: little children awaiting a parade, my oldest daughter awaiting and anticipating her wedding day. Or my own delighted anticipation of my birthday celebrations, when I start reminding my children a month ahead of time to start saving their money to buy me lots of presents!

Keeping watch. Waiting. They are hard to do.

We don't know how long Simeon had been waiting. His story is told only in the Gospel of Luke, and Luke doesn't give us his age. We assume he was old, because surely he had waited faithfully and an angel had told him that he would not see death until he saw the Christ. He was not necessarily old, however, except in his faithfulness in keeping watch. In this he was a model for all ages—timeless and perfect.

I sometimes wonder why the writer of Hebrews didn't record Simeon as one of the heroes of faith in that great, triumphal listing in chapter 11. But maybe that is right. Maybe he was on the edge of that "great cloud of witnesses" (Hebrews 12:1). He was not Abel, the giver of a right sacrifice, nor was he Enoch, translated to heaven past death's doors. Simeon did in fact die. Nor was he Abraham, father of the earthly kingdom of God. Nor Noah, nor Moses, nor any one of these heroes of faith that stagger the mind with the testimonies of their lives.

No, Simeon is too much like any one of *us*, called faithfully to keep watch, to wait the days of his life for evidence of God's "consolation." How often we yearn, in our night watches, for that consolation also. And in doing so, yearn to be like Simeon—"righteous and devout."

But here is the heart of the story, the very event that gladdens our hearts in the deep night watch: Simeon's waiting *was requited.*

Eight days after Jesus' birth, his parents, as faithful Jews, had him circumcised, whereupon the name given by the angel before he was ever conceived—Jesus—was officially conferred. And Mary and Joseph made their way to the temple after the period of "purification" to offer a sacrifice of praise and to dedicate their son to the Lord. They wanted to do this all carefully according to the law.

But there was one minor problem. Mary and Joseph were dirt poor. This carpenter couple had probably spent their last dime just traveling from Nazareth to Bethlehem to Jerusalem. Leviticus 12, which specifies the law in this circumstance, requires a sacrifice of "a year-old lamb for a burnt offering, and a young pigeon or a dove for a sin offering" (v. 6). Even here, however, grace supplants the law, for if the couple was impoverished, as Jesus' parents were, the offering could be satisfied by "two doves or two young pigeons," one for the burnt offering, the other for the sin offering (v. 8).

Grace meets the requirement of the law. How pointed. Here Jesus comes, the very one whose grace will meet all the requirements of the law for our sin—the perfect and eternal sacrifice.

But there was also grace abundant in Simeon's long watch keeping. He knew nothing of these earthshaking events taking place in the dusty stable and in the streets. He was keeping watch, still faithful. What was the grace for Simeon?

It came to him in that quietest of voices, that soft voice of such fierce tenderness and terrible love, the whisperings of the Holy Spirit. Surely it comes to others who wait also. Those who spend the night watching and waiting for a son or daughter may very well not find an immediate answer, but they can know they are not waiting alone when the Holy Spirit whispers, "Jesus has come."

I kept watch by my mother's deathbed, night after night until the night of her dying, but the Holy Spirit was there, murmuring in my heart, "Jesus has come." And because of that, I know that heaven is a brighter place today for having my mother there. This is the way it came to Simeon. The Holy Spirit told him, "Jesus has come. The waiting has ended. You were never alone."

Simeon got up and went to the temple where he met—where he *held!*—this Jesus who came. And he did the right thing. For a God-fearing Jew or a perplexed Christian today, he did the right thing. He burst into song. Joy had come, as King David promised, in the morning after the long darkness of his waiting. Simeon sang! After all, more was received than was promised. He didn't just *see* Jesus, he *held* him in his arms—that close and real and powerful. No wonder Simeon sang.

And what a beautiful song this Nunc Dimittis is, for it is sung not just to Mary and Joseph and Jesus, but to us. Listen to what Simeon sang, there in the temple to our ears.

First, he proclaimed his own peace: "Now dismiss thy servant in peace." Simeon affirmed the end of the watch, but more than that he affirmed his own absolute peace in both watch keeping and in the end of the wait. It was all worth it! Why? To hold this Jesus next to his heart. This was the consolation of his soul.

In this life we will never escape the hard watch. We will spend long nights wondering where a loved one is, watching for his or her return. We will sit beside the hospital bed, heads held in disconsolate hands, wondering with hearts twisted by agony, how long. Each of us keeps watch, in his or her own way. Such suffering is unavoidable in this life, whether it is the illness slowly, intractably eroding the health of a young husband, the grief of a loved one's intractable plunge into sin, or the anguish of our own unremitting loneliness. But, like Simeon, we can hold the *consolation* of Israel—and of all of us—to our breast and find his peace infiltrating those wounds in our life as we keep watch. At the end of our wait, as for Simeon, lies the perfect peace of "our salvation." It is here, now, at this place where I keep watch.

Simeon burst into song, grateful after the long wait for the restoration of peace. He also saw the vindication for his watch keeping, for this child, this light penetrating the long night of his waiting, would be "a light for revelation to the Gentiles and for glory to [the] people Israel."

When peace in the form of Jesus' presence, with the incandescent leading of the Holy Spirit, infiltrates the gray uncertainty of any moment in our lives, it never simply burns inward. If we let that happen, harboring the revelation for our own sake, the light diminishes, the fire flickers out. If we let it burn outward, we become instead, light bearers, vessels of God's peace to a world in darkness.

Simeon's vision turned transcendently outward. It was a song of victory, a triumphant proclamation of joy: "Look! The Savior has come. Not only has he given *me* peace, but here is what he can do for you. He is a light in the darkness, the one that all of you, from your own lonely watchtowers, have been waiting for. More than this, he is a light for glory. This is not only a little baby; this is the King of Creation."

Simeon, then, rejoiced in his peace, proclaimed a triumphant vision of Jesus' glory, and then provided promises. What a tender moment it was when he looked into the eyes of Mary, this eager young mother. How meaningful his blessing must have been to her, bewildered as she was in this strange city. So, still holding the baby, he turned from himself and from his vision of glory, and turned to Mary and Joseph, and blessed them with their child.

But the blessing is unsettling. To Mary he said, "This child is destined to cause the falling and rising of many in Israel." Yes, indeed, the mighty and prepossessing would fall before the world ruler. And many unexpected ones, some lowly fishermen, a tax collector, a prostitute, the unlikely and unlovely ones, would rise under his reign of grace. If the blessing was unsettling, it was also accompanied by the reality of future pain, for Simeon foresaw that this child was also the one who would become the perfect, final sacrifice. Not only would a sword pierce Jesus' side on Calvary, but a sword of grief would pierce Mary's heart.

And our hearts too remain pierced. We may have the precious peace of Jesus' presence, we may receive the unquenchable light of his victorious reign, but these occur, for the time of our human lives, in a sin-beset world where pain is a daily reality. That is what makes the peace and the light so dramatically important. That is the dynamic heart of everything Simeon said. Jesus is present here and now, at this very moment of need. We may be lonely on the watchtowers. Perhaps all we see are the cracks of the desert, thorns instead of flowers, a thirsty land instead of milk and honey. Who can escape such watches if we are serious about the enactment of our faith in this world? For this world can be a bedeviled and bewildering place.

Etched in my mind like an engraving in marble is one night in early September 1994. We sat in the small living room of my parents' home—Dad in his chair by the reading lamp, Mother—too weak to sit up—lying on the sofa. She was wearing, as always, a dress (I can't remember her in anything but a dress, many of which she made herself). She was wearing a sweater to ward off the constant chill, even though this night was quite warm. And I sat across from them, facing one of the hardest tasks a son can ever face. You see, there had been glitches in the flurry of treatments and procedures and records, things that should never happen but sometimes do, human error that led one doctor to tell Mother that there wasn't a trace of cancer left, that she was now fully in remission. My parents, of course, rejoiced.

As my wife and I quietly pursued her records further, we discovered the error, and it was left to me to tell them that not only was the cancer not in remission, but in spite of all the treatments it had grown more virulent. And as I did so, Mother looked at me. Her eyes were quiet, peaceful. I believe she already knew. She asked me, "Do they say how long I'll live?" And I answered precisely as the doctor had told me, "No, Mom. Perhaps a couple of months." But I wish now that I had given her another answer. One that is more certain, more true. "Forever, Mom. Forever."

But I think she knew that also.

The heart of Simeon's message also keeps beating in our age. In the anguish there is a peace. In the desert night there is a light. Through Jesus that peace and light stand within and all around you. But it is not isolated to our age; it shines forever.

For Further Study

Read Luke 2:21-35

1. It is important to bear in mind the humanity of the story of Simeon. It is not some distantly remote tale culled from the dry pages of history. Imagine yourself holding an eight-day-old baby. Imagine that this baby is very precious to you, one you have longed to see and hold. And now the time comes when you reach out your arms and cradle the infant. Now we get a

clearer sense of Simeon's excitement.

2. While we share Simeon's excitement, some of us also find that "keeping watch is so often an agony of uncertainty." Give specific or personal examples of how this is true.

3. Luke 2:25 tells us that Simeon was waiting "for the consolation of Israel." The word *consolation* comes from the Latin word for comfort. How was Jesus a comfort for Israel? How is he our comfort or solace today?

4. In what ways do we, like Simeon, hold the consolation of Israel? What lessons do we learn from Simeon about what we do with it?

5. Look closely at Simeon's benediction and promise in verses 34 and 35. How do you think they apply to us today?

Prayer

Now, Lord, I come to you for consolation. On my knees and broken I pray that you will cradle and comfort me. Hold me close. Still the beating of my fearful heart when I become honest with you. Let me know that I am safe, just as I am, because you love me. Amen.

9

The Outstretched
Arms of God
ANNA

*T*HE TEMPLE REPRESENTED THE CENTRALITY OF JEWISH NATIONAL identity in much the same way that the national flag does for Americans. The difference is that the temple for the Jews also held a vertical symbolism absent from the American flag. For them, the temple was the place where God revealed himself, and a place where the people could come to God. It was the central link in a vertical chain between the lowliest Jew and the most high God.

It was here in the temple that Anna, the prophetess, made her home and kept watch. If there was to be a revelation, it would happen here, at this sacred spot.

But the sacred spot had deteriorated significantly since it had first been instituted. History had not been kind to the temple.

The temple itself, as a central place of worship, had been instituted as the tabernacle of Moses' time. Constructed during the exodus, the tabernacle was a richly and ornately designed work, embellished with elaborate artwork and holding the most precious spiritual treasures of the people. The sacred Ark of the Covenant, residing in the Holy of Holies, wasn't merely a symbol of God's presence—it held the presence of God.

When the people crossed into Canaan, the tabernacle was more permanently situated, but it wasn't until the rule of King Solomon, almost a thousand years before Jesus was born, that the permanent structure of the tabernacle, now called the temple, was built. This building was about twice as large as the tabernacle, but the glory seemed to have turned inside out. In the tabernacle, the decorations turned even more glorious the deeper in one went, until finally one arrived at the Holy of Holies. The temple, on the other hand, had its most shining and stunning works on the outside.

There is a very subtle transition here simply in the architecture of two structures. One pulled the believer deeper into the mysterious experience of God; the other showed to anyone passing by that this is what God has done for his people.

Still, it was a powerful display of God's riches to his people, his power in the land, and Solomon's devotion.

But it was not the kind of temple where Anna kept watch.

In the years following Solomon's reign, the kingdom experienced a general, widespread spiritual decay. It was like a crack widening in the foundation of belief. Instead of traveling to the central temple, groups of people began building their own little temples out in the back reaches of the land, and fell out of touch with that central place. Later kings themselves lost the sense of sacredness. They saw the treasures kept there and used them for their own ends, gradually stripping the temple to aesthetic nakedness. In time they just didn't care. So when marauders came first to desecrate the temple, then destroy it, few cared enough to defend it. It was probably at this period in history, with its flagrant and violent looting of the temple, that the Ark of the Covenant was lost.

It was as if God had disappeared from the midst of the people. Now there was only this structure, this building, contested over by men for the few baubles it still contained.

During the exile and in later years God's people made several attempts to reconstruct the temple. But the nature of the building itself seemed to change. Gradually it turned into a military fortress, rather than a house of God. And we find a nearly complete reversal: from a place where people came to meet God to a place designed to keep people out.

So too it would have kept Anna out, save for one final change in the story.

About twenty years before Jesus was born, King Herod came up with a shrewd political move. By no means was his reconstruction motivated by religious conviction. *If I were to reconstruct this people's temple,* he reasoned, *then surely their loyalty would go to me—their benefactor—first of all.* And so he undertook a mammoth project at a truly astonishing pace. The structure as a whole was not completed until A.D. 64, but by 9 B.C. much of the basic structure had been built. Its courts, its rooms and porches, its altar—all these were in place.

It was into this temple that Anna the prophetess moved. And there she stayed. As Luke puts it, "She never left the temple but worshiped night and day, fasting and praying" (2:37). Like Simeon, she waited for the consolation of Israel, the light for revelation to the Gentiles. She was one of the faithful ones. One keeping faithful watch.

We only know two bits of information about Anna with complete certainty: her age and her marital status.

Anna was elderly, at least eighty-seven, maybe more depending on how one calculates the dating in Luke 2. A very old woman for her historical context.

Something in us—do we dare this honesty?—makes us recoil slightly from the very old. Perhaps it is the reminder of our own mortality. Wrinkled flesh and diminished faculties are a sign to ourselves of our own end. Careful of step, selective of words, the very old seem always on guard. We do not want to be like them. And perhaps especially not like Anna, who spent the last years of her life huddled in the temple, a place she was barely tolerated, while she fasted and prayed day and night. The picture is too much like dereliction rather than nobility. Give us another hero, Luke. We don't understand this one—she's too old, too lonely, too wasted by age and fasting.

And yet, as when we come to know the very old, and as we come to know Anna beyond the rituals she kept, we discover a nobility belied by wrinkled skin and thinning hair and groaning limbs. These elderly have stories. They carry the past on stooped shoulders. Each callus on her wrinkled hands—go ahead, reach out and touch them—recalls a success or a failure, worn spots in the very humanity of the person.

We do well to listen to Anna keeping watch in the temple, for hers is a story of love.

The second fact we know about Anna is that she was a widow. If we understand from Luke 2 that she was married only seven years, she had been a widow for a very long time. So long that Luke records her lineage through her father Phanuel rather than through any associations with her husband.

But, as is so often typical of Luke's writing, a very subtle twist occurs in the story of Anna and her father, for Phanuel is identified as being of the tribe of Asher. If we remember the story in the Old Testament, Asher was the eighth son of Jacob, himself the patriarch of the tribe of Asher. Just before the Israelites enter the Promised Land after their long sojourn in the desert, Moses blesses them tribe by tribe. Of Asher he says: "Most blessed of sons is Asher; let him be favored by his brothers, and let him bathe his feet in oil" (Deuteronomy 33:24). The blessing must have been unusual yet hopeful to this tribe. In the desert there had been little olive oil, yet they were promised it in abundance in their new land. Not only would they have sufficient oil for anointing, they would have so much they could wash their feet in it if they chose.

The tribe of Asher, as the Israelites spread out in the Promised Land, settled in a coastal area of western Galilee, an area that would become famous for its production of highest quality olive oil. This would be the oil for anointing kings. Such was their fame, until the huge unsettling of the exile. People were uprooted from ancestral lands, old customs were abolished, relationships and lineages lost. Save for Anna.

She arrived at the temple representing the richest oil of her people, to be poured out in a spiritual love offering on her king.

But she had no oil in her hands. Nothing but herself could she bring. As she heard Simeon's marvelous song, she came forward ("at that very hour"), gave thanks to God and began to tell others that the Messiah had come.

Perhaps each of us understands love in personal terms rather than in exemplary forms by others. That is, not until we have had our own hearts quicken with the thought of someone else, our breath catch for a moment at the sight of someone else—knowing these inward experiences—do we form a basis for understanding a deeper, more powerful love. We have to grow into that love that is sacrificial, seeing not what one does for my pulse rate, but what I can do for another. We have to grow into that love that roots deep in the spirit, at that place where trust and safety lie. We have to learn that love that waits, rather than the passion that requires satisfaction.

Such a love Anna had.

We learn about such love from personal experience, surely. We learn about it very often from the example of others. Their devotion sets a course for our own; their faithfulness embodies a model for our own. Anna provides one such example.

Another appears in Toni Morrison's Pulitzer Prize-winning novel, *Beloved* (Plume, 1988). It is a novel about ways of loving. The story takes place in the years immediately during and following the Civil War. It features three main characters: Sethe, the plantation house slave who, while pregnant, escaped to Ohio with her children; Paul D who was sold downriver, escaped to the North and rejoined Sethe eighteen years later; and Baby Suggs, the aged mother-in-law of Sethe. Sethe's husband, Halle Suggs, went insane under the new plantation owner and is presumably dead.

Each of these characters, raised on a plantation where it was dangerous to love because the slaves had no permanence and no control over their love, has to learn to love all over again in freedom.

Baby Suggs, the ex-slave whose freedom was purchased by her son Halle, teaches other ex-slaves in the free state of Ohio to love themselves. She is called the Holy Woman, for she spreads a gospel of the holiness of self love: "Love your hands! Love them. Raise them up and kiss them. Touch others with them, put them together, stroke them on your face" (p. 88). Baby Suggs and other former slaves were depreciated as of no worth under slavery; they were cattle—bought and sold and used. Now they must learn to love their own worth in order to love others. "O my people," says Baby Suggs, "hear me, they do not love your neck unnoosed and straight. So love your neck."

Paul D, the runaway slave who was led back with a bit in his mouth, who was held captive in a small, zoolike box, who wandered for eighteen years in search of something steadfast, has learned to love small. His heart withdraws, shrinks inward. The pain of the past seems so much greater than whatever hope the future holds. "The best thing, he knew, was to love just a little bit; everything, just a little bit, so when they broke its back, or shoved it in a croaker sack, well, maybe you'd have a little love left over for the next one" (p. 45). For Paul D, a person has only so much love; it has to be guarded carefully, given in small amounts so the heart isn't thoroughly shipwrecked against the rocks of inevitable loss. The ex-slave measures his life in what he has lost, rather than gained, and the amount of love is ever diminishing. The very ability to love, in his estimation, is the essential definition of freedom: "To get to a place where you could love anything you chose—not to need permission for desire—well now, *that* was freedom" (p. 162).

This is what Paul D believes until, after eighteen years, he finds Sethe, one of the loved ones taken from him. Slavery was a vicious, cruel game, in which children of God were the "things" won or lost. No one stops playing with the puzzle, even when the pieces are your children. Because she loves her children, and wants freedom for them, Sethe's love is moved by huge risks. She will do anything in the name of love; so fierce is her devotion that she will kill or be killed.

Sethe took it upon her own narrow shoulders to escape with her children, for "I stretched out my arms and all my children could get in between. I was *that* wide" (p. 162). On the plantation in Kentucky, Sethe found that she couldn't love them properly "because they wasn't mine to love." Not until she crossed that great divide of the Ohio River did she discover "there wasn't nobody in the world I couldn't love if I wanted to." Such love breeds pain, surely. Such love also liberates, as it gives identity to others.

Consider the love of Anna. She was a very old woman, unlovely to worldly eyes. She kept watch day and night in a place where she was not welcome. In Herod's temple women had a special court, set apart. They were not part of temple life, nor of political life. Women and children together had less vote than one man. Women like Anna didn't count to others. But they counted with Jesus.

Anna was not enslaved, but she was chained by her status. The peculiar horror of the slavery that held Baby Suggs, Paul D and Sethe must never be discounted, but there is another slavery that holds all humanity in bondage. Its chains are internal and wrap around our hearts. It is the very reason we wait like Anna for "the consolation of Israel," the bondage breaker who comes to people who don't seem to count for much.

If we dare to find ourselves there, at the threshold between slavery and freedom, we also count the terrible cost. This is no Ohio River that we can swim or boat across to freedom. It is a river wide and deep as the east is from the west. The passage of our going may only be paid in love.

So here is the terrible risk of the bondage-breaker, this "consolation of Israel." He too "stretched out [his] arms and all [his] children could get in between." Jesus is *that* wide. His arms were pinioned like an eagle's wings, stretched wide on the cross so that we, in the words of Isaiah, "soar on wings like eagles" from the bondage that enslaves us. *That* wide, he stretched his arms, gathering all his children in between and holding them protectively around his heart.

Renewed in such a way, and only in such a way, can we begin to love others truly. It is not the way of human love, our earthly love. In ourselves our quest for love is like digging for treasure in a field of stone. Sometimes we receive requital; too often we receive a pain that lingers the rest of our lives. It is a love that passes like the whisper of the wind on a cloudy day. We touch it briefly, then it is irretrievably gone, lost somewhere in the clouds that move like rudderless ships across the sky.

But Anna sought—for eighty-seven years—a love that held fast. Anchored in time and for all time to come. If we find that love between the arms of Jesus—"Just come in," Anna might tell us; "let him hold you"—it colors the way we see others. We aren't about the task of seeing what we can *get* from them, but what we can *give.* There is no room for hostility, for we are free. "Love your hands," says Baby Suggs. Why? Because only by loving ourselves truly—as children wrapped between the arms of Jesus—do we begin loving others truly.

What we seldom realize is that the well-known words of John 3:16, "For God so loved the world that he gave his one and only Son that whoever believes in him shall not perish but have eternal life," are not simply past tense words. They are present and future words as well. Because God loved the world, we can and must love the world. Because God gave his one and only Son, we can and must give of ourselves to this world. Because we believe in the Son as Redeemer, we can and must, in all tenderness, power and loving devotion, rescue the perishing.

And this is what Anna did. She waited, day and night. And when the infant appeared, baby arms flailing about, stretching and closing, she witnessed the Truth enfleshed. And she went out of the temple and told everyone she could.

For Further Study

Read Luke 2:36-38

1. The temple of Solomon had been devastated, destroyed and rebuilt many times by the time Jesus was born. In fact, at the time of his birth it was being rebuilt. To distinguish the temple from our modern churches, it is helpful to glance over chapters 3—5 of 2 Chronicles. There we see the

separate areas and degrees of holiness associated with them. How might this compare (or contrast) with your church?

2. We might also compare the many attacks on the temple to the attacks on today's church. What are the greatest threats to the church today? Do they arise from the outside or from within?

3. Anna came from a region rich in olive oil, which was used symbolically and religiously by the Jewish nation. What did Anna bring instead? Were her waiting and watchkeeping themselves offerings to Jesus?

4. How does the story of Toni Morrison's *Beloved* exemplify Anna? What lessons might it provide for us?

5. What is the essential starting point for loving ourselves? for loving others? What prevents us from loving in such a way? Matthew 6:19-21 and 2 Corinthians 4:5-7 are helpful here. What did Anna do when her waiting was fulfilled?

Prayer

Anna leaves me breathless and bewildered, Lord. What faithfulness! I grow impatient in minutes. She kept watch for a lifetime. Yet how powerfully you rewarded her. Teach me just a bit of that patience, I pray. Help my heart to be still, to wait on you, knowing with absolute conviction that you, the God of eternity, work your lovingkindness in the minutes and days of my life. Amen.

10

Celebration
of Warriors
GOD'S ANGELS

*I*WAS QUITE SURPRISED WHEN I WAS CLEANING OUT AN OLD FILE IN MY office recently and read some words I had written long ago. About every five to seven years the college where I am employed requires a review of tenured teaching faculty. The file represented my turn for review, an arduous and challenging process. Recommendations have to be gathered from current students, from alumni, from colleagues, from scholars in the major field of the instructor. Board members and colleagues visit classes. Evaluation forms multiply faster than cockroaches. Then, finally, the instructor has to write a fairly lengthy essay responding to various sets of questions.

About the time I was nearing the finish, I was ready to look for a new job. I had just one answer left to respond to, and it was the one that stumped me: "What are your goals for the next five years?" It led to the words on that page I rediscovered. Some people, I'm sure, have their lives planned out that far in advance. I don't. Generally I have more than enough to do today and am content with what God will give me tomorrow. In today's regimented world that's probably a bad attitude. Nonetheless, it's mine. So I responded to the question the way I would to an issue on the editorial page, fully expecting it to wind up wadded in the waste basket. But when I couldn't think of anything better to say, I sent the statement in anyway.

The sheet I found in the file had fifteen items. I'll give only a few to give you an idea of its contents:

1. I want to be a good husband and father.

2. I'd like to find a fishing hole in Michigan as good as the ones I had in Pennsylvania and Ohio.

5. I would like just once to beat my wife at tennis. I mean trounce her for three sets.

7. I would like to develop the best kill shot in racquetball in western Michigan.

10. In five years I'd like to work in my garden just as I do now.

13. Within the next five years I'd like to meet an angel. And have him identify himself as such.

A certain poignancy attaches to that last item. Here is another secret I have not kept well hidden. For some odd reason, ever since I was a little boy listening to my first Bible stories, I have had a burning desire to see an angel. I'm full of questions I would want to ask him, but mostly I wonder what he would look like. Would he be like a white, flaming light? Like those angels that danced in the sky over the shepherds, celebrating the birth of Jesus? Or, would he come as a common passerby, like the three men who visited Abraham under the oaks of Mamre? Maybe I have met an angel, unaware of the fact, as Hebrews 13:2 advises. If so, I wish he had told me before leaving.

Of one thing I'm certain. Angels are very little like those the cults of angelology champion today. In fact, someone like myself, who has long had an almost mystical fascination with the angels of the Bible, tends to get irritated rather quickly with the cutesy, good luck charm attitude some popular celebrities and a host of plain people have toward angels. A case in point. At one time during the inexorably protracted O. J. Simpson trial, Denise Brown drew attention to her angel pin and angel earrings. Soon similarly crass jewelry was being peddled in return for donations to certain causes. How charming. An angel of genuine sterling silver set on a pin. How shocking should one of the majestic envoys from God's throne, clad in light and thundering with power, appear to a purchaser. Even the most striking angel pin merely demonstrates how thoroughly the human imagination can diminish God's magnificent creation.

I am reminded of how many times, in their manifestations recorded biblically, the first words of angels are "Don't be afraid." And they refuse to let humans worship them. Even that tendency toward worship and fear is telling. The angels don't dance on center stage, sucking up the floodlights. They serve God and want us to get excited about God.

But the human imagination can afford us a glimpse of heavenly majesty. Witness C. S. Lewis's description in *Perelandra* where Ransom meets the great Oyarsa through a stream of light. Ransom's reaction, I believe, would be very much like my own: "Oyarsa passed between his subjects and drew near and came to rest, not ten yards away from Ransom in the center of Meldilorn. Ransom felt a tingling of his blood and a pricking on his fingers as if lightning were near him; and his heart and body seemed to him to be made of water." It is both a feeling of absolute terror and also terrifying safety. Ransom is in the presence of power beyond human imagination—a power held by a messenger from the throne of God.

It does seem that with angels we are caught on the cusp of our unknowing. We rely on the imagination to fill in what we don't know. Often human imagination detours us into a dark jungle of errors; at other times it reveals dazzling flashes of insight.

During the last half dozen years, as celebrities and such quasi-religious movements as New Ageism have embraced the cult of angelology, there have probably been several dozen books published on angels. These range from pseudomyths by venial charlatans to excellent theological studies by respected Christian authors. I must confess that I have not read them. I don't want to lose my sense of awe and wonder before the majestic creations. I'm still trying to peek under the wrinkled edges of the Christmas wrapping paper, trying to see if what I have long imagined is indeed true. And I wonder if wonder isn't the best response to this splendid gift of God.

In fact, the only book on angels that I have read cover to cover is the Bible.

Angels in the Bible

How can the Bible guide our fragile imaginations here so that we can rightly understand the angels and particularly that great messenger, this divine agent Gabriel, whose joy and glory it was to announce the Redeemer's birth? The Bible can remind us of the roles that God's angels play in our lives. The tasks he has given them are, after all, quite different from the human-generated and cultic claims we hear all around us in a world that markets angels like Disney World souvenirs.

Just as we identify each other by physical characteristics (Shaquille O'Neal is 7'1" and weighs 303 pounds) and occupations (Shaquille O'Neal plays basketball), so too we have identifying information about angels from the Bible. Several items may be mentioned quickly to establish identity. First, there is a vast number of them. David saw thousands of them with God's chariots (Psalm 68:17). Ten thousand appeared at Mount Sinai (Deuteronomy 33:2). John tells us that ten thousand times ten thousand minister before God (Revelation 5:11). Their numbers are literally innumerable by humans (Hebrews 12:22).

Although there is a staggering number of angels, they share, like the staggering number of humans, certain fundamental traits. They are created, not eternal. They are spirits, and therefore immortal, not resurrected. They can appear in human form, and speak human languages, but unlike humans they neither marry nor beget children. Unlike humans, they have unimaginable power; unlike God, they are not omnipotent. Nor are they all-knowing. They are often messengers from God's throne, but God designs the message.

Perhaps this should be added in this matter of definition: there are good angels and evil or fallen angels. Those fallen angels, as 2 Peter 2:4 and Jude 6 put it, revolted against God in heaven, were cast out and "committed to pits of nether gloom to be kept until the judgment"

(RSV). Whether this is a present or future state is debatable. Clearly Satan roams the earth like a roaring lion seeking whom he may devour; clearly also ongoing angelic warfare is recorded in the Bible. In Daniel 10, Daniel learns that the great archangel Michael assisted another angel in a twenty-one-day battle against the "prince of Persia" (v. 13). Whatever the case, God's armies of angels vanquished the rebellious host.

John Milton was physically blind, but his imaginative vision was never keener than when he wrote the dramatic Book 6 of *Paradise Lost.* By the power of his language he takes us to the raging landscape of heaven, legion arrayed against legion. At the defeat of the evil ones, "Hell at last / Yawning received them whole, and on them closed, / Hell, their fit habitation, fraught with fire / Unquenchable, the house of woe and pain" (11.874-77). Milton's vision is also reality; God and his angels do rule supreme over all the hideous forces and manipulative tricks of Satan and his demons.

Warriors

This conquering power of God's angels is not limited to the war in heaven. There is an ongoing warfare here on earth. Many instances of angelic war upon evil are recorded in the Bible. For example, Genesis 19 records that God sent two angels to destroy Sodom, a city so saturated with evil that only a rage of flames could cleanse it. In the New Testament Jesus makes clear that angelic powers will rout evil. Explaining his parable of the sower to his disciples, Jesus said of the weeds, "the enemy who sows them is the devil. The harvest is the close of the age, and the harvesters are angels" (Matthew 13:39). Above all, however, Jesus has final authority. It is at his word alone, like a breath of undeniable power, that the evil angels will finally be caged: "Then he will say to those on his left, 'Depart from me, you who are cursed, into the eternal fire prepared for the devil and his angels' " (Matthew 25:41).

Believers, however, do not simply defer this battle to the angels. We have to ask, To what end is the battle? It is not warfare without purpose or direction, nor simply an ongoing skirmish between powers and principalities to which we can live in blissful oblivion. If we simply sit back and count our blessings one by one, raising up our songs of how it is well with our souls when souls are being dragged to hell by the chuckling demons, then we have failed terribly, you and I.

In one of his many calls for revival, the great nineteenth-century preacher Charles Spurgeon encouraged his listeners to a renewed godliness and a warfare of sound doctrine. His fear was that the church "has begun to be honored in the eyes of the world. The Church must be despised and cast out until the Lord comes, in whose eyes we are to find true honor." While we could hardly say that the contemporary church is held in honor by the world, Spurgeon's point still applies. It is when the church is of no offense or consequence to the world that we believers are in deep spiritual trouble. Our battle lines, like those of God's angels, are clearly drawn. We don't just sit back and *let* them fight for us. They are our allies, fighting with and for us.

So too we are keeping watch. This is never, ever, a matter of passive waiting. Keeping watch is an active work. We stand like sentinels on the watchtower. Our eyes are sharp, our spirits ready. As we keep watch we recognize, furthermore, that the warfare against evil is not only with the angels; it is with the very one for whom we keep watch. The angels are the Lord's agents. As Jesus drove back evil, creating huge areas of safe ground, so too he joins us with his mighty army to bring others to safety.

The key point here is that Jesus also requited the demands of the evil one for our sake. We are bought with a price, not of gold but of divine blood. Even at that final moment, Jesus told his disciples, "Do you think I cannot call on my Father, and he will at once put at my disposal more than twelve legions of angels?" (Matthew 26:53). So he could have done, scouring the earth clean. But Jesus adds, "How then would the Scriptures be fulfilled?" (v. 54). In this way, Jesus himself kept watch. His eye was on his Father in obedience, but also surely on us in love.

Protectors

We should understand, moreover, that angels not only engage in warfare *against* evil but also protect believers *from* evil. In fact, this task is probably the one most frequently mentioned in Scripture. King David powerfully and repeatedly testifies to this protective work in his psalms. "The angel of the Lord encamps around those who fear him, and delivers them," he asserts in Psalm 34:7. And again, in Psalm 91:11, we find these familiar and reassuring words: "For he will command his angels concerning you to guard you in all your ways."

While David provides some of the most familiar testimony to the angels' protection, that task is clearly established long before. When Abraham sent his servant in search of a wife for Isaac, he promised that God would "send his angel before [him]" (Genesis 24:7). Similarly, when the Israelites were camped in Sinai following their exodus and were about to cross over into the Promised Land, which was nonetheless peopled by enemies of God, God promised Moses, "See, I am sending an angel ahead of you to guard you along the way and to bring you to the place I have prepared" (Exodus 23:20).

The pattern certainly prevails into the New Testament. Consider Paul's last missionary journey to Rome. It was a rough passage from the start, the ship awkward and blown off course in the seething water. As the storm grew into a tempest, the ship was helplessly foundering, blown by every whim of wind. For fourteen days the storm raged. As the crew members gave themselves up for lost, Paul stood up to encourage them. He had good reason: "Last night an angel of God whose I am and whom I serve stood beside me" (Acts 27:23). The angel's message to Paul? Do not fear. God is in control.

Paul's tempest was actual; many of ours are metaphorical—but nonetheless perilous. Indeed there are moments when the course of our lives seems shipwrecked, when there is no one at the helm, and when indiscriminate winds toss us everywhere but toward a safe harbor. But here there is another master, the same who spoke to the waves of the Sea of Galilee, "Peace, be still." In the same authority, Jesus tells us, "I will not leave you desolate; I will come to you" (John 14:18 RSV). What the angels achieve, Jesus authorizes. The protection they provide comes at his command. The protective power of the angels prevails as we abide in Christ.

Our first-born son was the kind of baby every parent dreams of—happy, playful, good-natured. Best of all, he fell asleep in seconds and stayed sound asleep all night.

No doubt, he was the easiest of our four children as a baby. At least until he arrived at the age of four. Suddenly, for some reason we never understood, he would lie awake long into the darkness, unsettled and frightened.

So it was one night that I happened to be standing in the hallway while my wife spoke words of comfort into Jeff's ear. I listened to her work of tenderness. I peeked into the doorway, and, by the dim light of the Sesame Street night-light, saw her kneeling by his bed, speaking these words.

"Jeff," she said, "you know you don't have to be afraid. You know that God loves you."

Jeff nodded and muttered something I couldn't hear.

"And you know," Pat added, "that his Holy Spirit lives in us."

"Okay," said Jeff. His voice sounded sleepy. He yawned.

"And Jesus loves you very, very much, and takes care of you."

Again he nodded. Slowly, as if he were drifting off.

And then Pat added, "And you know he gives his angels charge of you."

Jeff sat bolt upright. "Keep those guys away from me," he said loudly.

I hope he didn't notice me doubled up with silent laughter in the hall.

Thinking of that now, I believe that many of us are like four-year-old Jeff, somehow unsure about and indeed quite afraid of angels. We would just as soon keep those guys away from us. I'm sure many non-Christians would wish that too, if they knew the power angels bear. But not believers, for to us they are the powerful, protective agents of God, the means by which we often are, probably without our knowing it, "delivered from evil." That in itself is cause for celebration.

Celebrants

The early American Puritan church service—held in a "meeting house" of untreated lumber and kept at the same temperature as the outside—was not a place of merriment. Despite the fact that their *Bay Psalm Book* (distrusting "worldly" translations of the Psalms, they made their own) had used the verse "If any be happy, let him sing songs of praise" (James 5:13) as an epigraph, the Puritans' singing was a somber, atonal, unaccompanied exercise in drudgery. They had so many rules governing "Sabbath" observance, it's a wonder a person dared get out of bed in the morning—except that there was a rule against sloth. Yet, to get into this quirky enclave one had to testify, sometimes for hours, that one was "elect." And life thereafter consisted of a ceaseless process of self-examination for election.

Nonetheless, we find many things to admire in the Puritans: the extraordinary courage, the rootedness of all their life in God, the subjection of all life to God, the fierce moral integrity. These are all admirable, but one would hardly dare accuse them of being a joyful people. I wonder if, thereby, they didn't miss the very essence of the gospel.

Sometimes we make the mistake of viewing the angels as something akin to a Puritan elder—ever on the alert for wrongdoing, quick and forceful with retribution on errant humans. In effect, we see them as warriors and protectors, but hardly joyful celebrants.

I believe that view is wrong, and contrary to Scripture. I do not believe that angels are joyless creatures of scowling demeanor. They are victorious, powerful in their knowledge of King Jesus, ready to burst into victory celebration. And perhaps the greatest celebration occurred at the nativity of their king, because they too had been keeping watch for this moment when victory in the war against evil was decided.

In this matter of anticipation and celebration, the angel Gabriel played a special part. Already during the time of Daniel, Gabriel brought prophetic news of the coming Christ and his reign. Looking toward the end times, Gabriel described the rise of the antichrist and declared that the antichrist would "take his stand against the Prince of princes. Yet he will be destroyed, but not by human power" (Daniel 8:25).

Then the centuries turned until the time of the Prince of princes was at hand. We can scarcely imagine Gabriel's excitement during that series of visitations described in the first chapter of Luke. Consider the sequence; one can almost feel the hopes and anticipations of all generations past, and all those yet to come, buckling together here at God's appointed moment.

It must have seemed a day like any other to Zechariah; after all, as an aging priest he had been through this so very many times before. Perhaps the only thing that made it slightly different was that this time it was Zechariah who was chosen by lot from his division of priests to enter the inner temple and burn incense. Still, he had no cause to suspect he would find someone there waiting for him. But there by the altar of incense stood Gabriel. His message? You, Zechariah, and your wife Elizabeth will have a son, and he will play a vital role in events soon to unfold. As Isaiah prophesied, his task will be "to make ready a people prepared for the Lord" (Luke 1:17). It is unnecessary to detail Zechariah's bewilderment here, and his inability to speak until the child was born. The point is that Gabriel, at God's precise direction, was carefully knitting together the prophecies of those Old Testament watch keepers with events about to happen in Israel. But Gabriel had another divine visit to make.

It was during Elizabeth's sixth month of pregnancy that Gabriel appeared to the young virgin, Mary. The telling in Luke seems at first to put it so matter-of-factly: "Gabriel was sent from God to a city in Galilee named Nazareth." But how do we comprehend this? From the throne of Almighty God this angel is given an assignment: Tell them. It is time. And how Gabriel must have been bursting as he called out, "Greetings, you who are highly favored! The Lord is with you." He went on to say that the Lord was *in* her!

Gabriel was not alone in the celebration of the child's birth. There were human voices raised in praise—Mary's to be sure, but also those of Joseph and Elizabeth and Zechariah. To their praise a host of angels added their voices on the birth of the Promised One. The night sky rippled with their presence.

It is not a huge step to believe that these same angels, those who in Revelation shout their honor of the Lamb, join us in adoration and celebration. And if they join us in such a way, it makes all the more poignant the fact that we are part of a family—we transient but soon to be resurrected mortals and those timeless immortals. They are our stronger brothers, looking out for us, the children of God.

Keeping watch in the darkness, struggling against the attacks of Satan, the angels also give us a glimpse of the ecstatic joy that will one day be ours.

For Further Study

Read Luke 2:8-14; Matthew 26:52-54

1. Without reflecting too much, list some of the popular ideas about angels in our culture today. Now list some of the characteristics found in Scripture. For example, nearly every time an angel appears to a human, the first words are "Be not afraid." What qualities does that suggest?

2. Do you believe that angels are all around us? What passages in Scripture might support this? Angels are to be revered as God's ambassadors, but we have to be careful not to give them too much reverent attention. Study Hebrews 1 carefully. How does the passage make this very clear?

3. According to chapter ten, what specific tasks are given to angels? Think of other ideas found in Scripture.

4. How do we help the angels in the warfare against evil? One way is to resist the temptation to evil ourselves. List other specific ways this can be done.

5. Is there a conflict in seeing angels as both mighty warriors and joyful celebrants? What do they celebrate? What lessons can we learn from their celebration?

Prayer

I thank you, Lord, that your mighty angels are all around, but I am just as thankful that they lead me in a celebration of praise for the Lord of lords and King of kings. Will you take my fumbling words and faulty tunes and translate them into your choir of praise? Above all, touch my heart. May I feel some of the angelic joy over the newborn King in each moment of my life. Let that joy live on in me, I pray. Amen.

11

In from the Fields
THE
SHEPHERDS

*L*UKE STARTS THE SHEPHERDS' NARRATIVE IN STARK, NON-dramatic terms, "And there were shepherds living out in the field nearby, keeping watch over their flocks at night" (Luke 2:8).

Take note of what they were *not* watching for. They were not looking for any miracles; they had work of their own to do. They were not keeping watch for a Messiah to be born; they were concerned about any ewes ready to deliver. They were not at all concerned about the Lion of Judah. They listened only for the shuffle of the jackal.

Their job of sheepherding was almost as old as the nation of Israel itself; the methods and the demands had changed little in all that time. Even after the nomadic wanderings of the earlier years, sheep remained one of the most useful commodities in the settled villages, providing sacrifices, meat, wool, and horn implements.

The shepherd's task in meeting this need grew more difficult with the seasonal weather changes. In the spring, after the winter rains, flocks could be kept relatively close to the village, but as the hot sun blazed and the fields scorched, shepherds had to lead their charges long distances to find food on the stony ground. There in the wilds the sheep were susceptible to animals of prey, and shepherds would go armed with slings (like David) and "rods" or clubs. At night the shepherds would lead their flock to a safe place—a rude, natural sheepfold—and keep watch over them during the night hours.

Working in long weeks of isolation with his sheep, the good shepherd got to know their names and all their quirky habits. That knowledge was necessary also to be able to separate the sheep quickly into flocks should a buyer come. There was nothing romantic about shepherds. Their clothes grew ragged and stained with mud. They had to be attentive to the bull-headed old rams and the curious young lambs.

The customs and manners of a person's life, however, do little to give a true picture of that person. We may find this to be true even of our best and closest friends. That woman who sells donuts at the grocery store, with whom you pass polite conversation every so often, turns out to be the one who leads you through your grief because she herself has undergone the brutal trial of losing a loved one to cancer. Or that elder in the church, whom you had believed to be as shallow as a puddle, turns out to be the one who, at your hour of despair, through repeated visits, charms your fears and quiets your heart.

In the same way, had we seen these shepherds with their rude manners, low customs and dirty clothes, we might have thought them unworthy of further notice. But God saw their true worth and had a surprise in store for them while they were keeping watch.

Life-Changing Glory

How very abruptly Luke puts it, as if to dramatize the contrast. Here in chapter 2, verse 8, the shepherds lounge about their nighttime duties, just keeping watch. It is stated as matter-of-factly as an airline schedule. Then, at the beginning of verse 9, there is this startling report: "An angel of the Lord appeared to them." These were hardy men, these shepherds. But not so hardy as to be foolish. This was no fox or jackal: this was an angel. Their hearts must have shivered in the springtime night. Like stones in a sack they must have felt the weight of "What have I done?" But then the celestial panorama acquires strength and depth, as if accelerating with the unbearable brightness of joy. The verse continues, "The glory of the Lord shone around them, and they were terrified." No place to run. Nowhere to hide. It's all around them, like a blanket of light settling and unsettling, dancing in waves about them. They had a perfect right to be filled with fear.

I wonder what the sheep were doing? Were they as panic-stricken as their watch keepers, now plunging hopelessly up and down stony gullies? Anything to get away! Or did they just go about their sheepish business, calmly chewing a few blades of grass, watching heaven unfold with their soft eyes wide? I rather think they just went on being sheeplike, while their keepers quaked in their sandals.

The angel spoke to the hearts of fear pounding in these shepherds: "Do not be not afraid." He saw them shaking like branches in the glorywind. Don't be afraid: this is not a bad thing the heavens crack open to tell you. The angel continued, "I bring you good news of great joy that will be for all the people" (Luke 2:10). And on those last words were established the essentials of Christian belief. The angel demonstrated what every follower of the Messiah would be called to do— carry the good news. This was the headline announcement: There is a light in the darkness, a light that illuminates the stony ground and that puts the most fearful heart at ease.

The angel explained: "Today in the town of David a Savior has been born to you; he is Christ the Lord" (Luke 2:11). Then the angel drew a kind of road map, telling them where to find the child who lay in a manger, wrapped in swaddling clothes. As if they had been awaiting that cue, a curtain was swept back on heaven and a multitude of heavenly hosts emerged. What a chorus! Their song was like a tempest of praise over the Judean fields: "Glory to God in the highest and on earth peace to men on whom his favor rests." God's favor rests on these rude shepherds who have been issued a special birth announcement? Surely there are hundreds of people with higher status in the area than these men smelling of sheep and campfires . . . and sheep! What's going on here?

We do know that the shepherds heard the message the angel gave, and that they responded to it immediately. They went in haste, Luke tells us, and arrived at the manger. They acted on revelation, and found what they sought. Furthermore, once the shepherds saw Jesus, they scrambled around telling others about the angels' revelation and their verification. All who heard it, wondered, says Luke. Does that mean they didn't go also? Well, I suppose a certain number of them had babies to nurse, and chores to do, and shops to close. Maybe even a few sheep to watch. Regardless, like the angels, the shepherds told the good news, then "returned, glorifying and praising God for all they had heard and seen, as it had been told them" (Luke 2:20). They returned to keeping watch.

What the Shepherds Tell Us

If the shepherds have a message or some meaning for us, then, it might be first of all in their willingness *to act in faith upon divine revelation.* You see, the world would have, and probably should have, called them irresponsible. Their task was to take care of their sheep. That was their livelihood and responsibility, not chasing angels.

Christians today have a revelation also; the first and central divine revelation is the Bible. It's easy to agree with this; it's much harder to act according to it. In *Fear and Trembling* (Penguin, 1985), Søren Kierkegaard marvels at the faith of Abraham, observing, "He left behind his world of understanding and took with him his faith" (p. 50). In much the same way, the shepherds exhibit an act of supreme faith, setting all worldly understanding aside to answer a divine calling.

For us, something isn't reasonable unless we understand it. Could we call the shepherds reasonable men? Well, they may have been unkempt and rough, but not *unreasonable.* That is, they were not contrary to reason, or insane. Well, perhaps, someone might argue, they had simply experienced a nighttime illusion. Maybe a meteor landed at their feet, and all that noise and light was interpreted by them as a message to get home to Bethlehem where they happened to take in a sideshow at a manger ("Hey, Maude. You'll never believe what I saw . . ."). Well, if so they were certainly unreasonable because their sheep were still out in the field.

Each of us, like the shepherds, is called to unreasonable acts of faithfulness that make sense only in the context of God's calling on our lives. Seldom are there moments when the heavens crack open and an angel gives specific instructions. In fact, some of us live under a thick and impenetrable blanket of darkness. Or we wander through the nighttime, all night, watching the constellations fade to nothingness under the brown light of dawn. What voice do we hear then?

It is the same one as always. The revelation has been given, not just to the shepherds but to each of us. Go to Bethlehem. Go quickly. Leave the things of this world behind. Stop keeping watch with worldly understanding, and watch with eyes of faith.

Our personal anguish is very real; it may, in fact, continue unabated. Kierkegaard observed this as he studied Abraham's story. He writes: "What is left out of the Abraham story is the anguish; for while I am under no obligation to money, to a son the father has the highest and most sacred of obligations" (p. 58). And I am mindful of this question, What would happen if I acted like Abraham? Or like the shepherds? If I defied all that religion, ethics and the law taught me in order to follow the word of God? Faith is precisely that undisguised passion that makes us follow the call to Bethlehem in defiance of all the world tells us. Do I tend my sheep, or listen to a voice from on high?

These shepherds listened. I don't think anything could have stopped them from going. Indeed, they went in a hurry, excited.

And I wonder, in the second lesson in keeping watch that we take from the shepherds, if any of them thought along the way, *Will I be welcomed there?* This is, after all, a royal event, albeit in a manger. They went to see a Messiah, and surely a few among them must have thought as they stumbled over the hills toward Bethlehem, *I'm not worthy to be there. I have nothing to bring.*

It's with this thought that I begin to feel very much like the shepherds. I am not like one of the wise men, bearing gifts and honors. I am a person of the back stretches of the land, dressed in rude clothing, and watching fearfully from the sidelines. But I know many others who feel the same way—that they are not worthy to approach God, and that they have nothing to bring should they come.

And so we stand frozen where we are.

If the shepherds had behaved responsibly, they should have stayed in the field with their sheep. If they had honored social conventions of the time, they also should have stayed in the fields. These were, after all, smelly, rough men, armed with their slings and clubs. They were on the wrong side of social graces. Their rules of etiquette went something like: if a fox attacks my sheep, the fox dies. Lowlifes. Outcasts. Wanderers whose roof over their heads was the moon and stars. They had no gifts for a king.

But the baby they came to visit lay not in a palace but a manger. And the shepherds had nothing to bring but themselves. And all that they were. Nothing else would suffice; no better gift could they bring. In pure audacious boldness they came: I was called; here I am.

The very moment we begin to think of all the deeds we have accomplished in Jesus' name and for his kingdom, at that moment we begin to turn away from Jesus and his kingdom. This matter of being a Christian is never a matter of what we *do*. Just doing is doing nothing. The shepherds show us it is a matter of wholehearted devotion. Deeds follow out of that love, as they did for the shepherds—they ran around telling everyone they could find what had happened.

The issue has two implications. First, I have heard many people say, "I am not worthy to be a Christian. I haven't really done anything for God." I'd like to respond: look to the shepherds. They had nothing to bring. But they went. Second, I have also met people who have, for one reason or another, let a wall of sin grow between them and God. They may have repented and received forgiveness, but the memory of the sin still rises like a dark monolith in their minds, blotting out the light of grace. I want to say, look to the shepherds. They came, running, just as they were.

But the chief point is this: The shepherds may have felt of no worth, but they found someone of infinite worth who bestows life everlasting. The shepherds may have carried a load of sin on that midnight run, but they found the glory of peace.

And so we too come, in our hands jars of clay that bear the stories of our lives. It is all that we need, all that is asked.

For Further Study

Read 1 Samuel 17:14-15; Psalm 23; Luke 2:8-20

1. Jesus was born in the lineage of David (see chapter two). What connections do you see among the three Scripture readings?

2. With all the modern conveniences of our lives it is hard to imagine the crude, nomadic life of the shepherds. Perhaps the closest analogy would be wilderness backpacking. Was there anything special about the lives of the shepherds that may have made them particularly open to the angels' appearance? That is, what is there about the shepherd's life itself that led these shepherds to ready acceptance?

3. How does the angels' announcement form "the essentials of Christian belief"?

4. What is the essential lesson for us in the shepherds' reaction to that announcement?

5. What does the example of Kierkegaard teach us about our personal faith?

Prayer

Lord, you yourself taught me to have faith like a simple child. I ask you for such faith. Let me unclutter my mind and just come to you. Help me with that—hearing your call and coming to answer. But above all, I thank you for opening your arms to receive me. Amen.

12

Mysterious
Strangers
THE MAGI

*I*N THE CHRISTIAN TRADITION THE MAGI HAVE ALMOST DIMINISHED to myth. Their story, recorded in so many children's books, now seems to belong to the world of reindeer and elves and Santa Claus rather than biblical revelation. Just one more set of mysterious strangers who wandered into the Christmas story.

Nothing could be farther from the truth. Their role in the Messiah's birth as a link between the anticipations of Old Testament people keeping watch and those people of Jesus' time keeping watch, sometimes with evil intent, is as powerful as any in the incarnation narrative.

To understand that large claim, as well as these mysterious strangers themselves, we need to probe a little and answer some questions.

Where Did They Come From?
Where first of all, did these wise men originate? The Matthew account tells us they were from the East—an accurate but rather ambiguous answer. In fact, they came from a long way in the East, all the way

from Babylon, through life-withering desert sun and cold blast of wintry mountain air, not to mention through doubt and bewilderment. These were no ordinary travelers—these mysterious strangers from the East. The wise men were not just keeping watch; they were earnestly and brave-heartedly seeking the Messiah—and that for a very long time. Depending on the route they took, the journey would have covered eight hundred to one thousand miles—by camel! And it could have lasted up to two years.

How do we measure such passion? How do we conceive of such outrageous hope in an age where we agonize over a red-light delay? These were, indeed, no ordinary travelers.

We must understand that the Arabian Desert that these men braved is not a resort area. Temperatures during the day soar to unbearable heat, the kind that seems to suck vital energy right out through the flesh. At night, under a sky as huge as all space, the cold descends, and the traveler huddles for warmth. There are stretches of stony ground as bleak as a moonscape; there are rolling waves of wind-driven sand that flay the flesh and make directions a maze. Day after day the Magi braved the torment, their minds whispering to them, "This is foolish! Let's turn back while we still can." But still they went on.

Who Were They?

If they came from the East (probably from Babylon in ancient Persia, according to most biblical scholars), who were these travelers? They were called "wise men," a common designation for astrologers, but they were far more than mere stargazers. The Magi descended from the ancient tribe of the Medes in Persia, a kind of royal priesthood not unlike the Levites among the tribes of Israel. Although some of their members ascended to political power, they acted primarily as priests, and their tasks reflected this. First, as "wise" men they were called on to interpret dreams. This was one of the most basic tasks of wise men in the ancient world. Since in many kingdoms the king was allied with divine powers, his dreams were understood as divine revelations. But wise men were needed to interpret the revelation. Second, and also since they held this ability to interpret dreams, the Magi were considered intermediaries with the gods. They were a people set apart because of their contact with the gods. Third, they were gifted with understanding astronomy, for it was generally believed that the gods revealed themselves through stars and planets. They were astrologers, interpreting the heavenly signs.

The tasks mentioned above represent three ways in which the Magi could make known their gods' will to rulers or people—as interpreters of dreams, as intermediaries with the gods and as readers of the heavens. But they also had a more human task. They were repositories, or librarians, of significant human events. They needed a record of the past, after all, to frame their directions for the future.

As such the Magi were a highly elevated people in the kingdom. These were no common slouches that hopped aboard secondhand, traded-in camels for their trip. They were a part of the royalty, even when they did not directly hold royal power. We think so often of the rude nativity scene in Bethlehem, the stable visited by the likes of shepherds, or the temple greeters like Anna and Simeon. These men from the East, although ragged and dusty with travel, were not unlike limousine-ferried celebrities, bearing rich gifts.

But, if they were indeed a people of the comfortable life, why on earth would they leave it behind for the terrible discomfort of the desert? That, my heart doesn't understand. How can we measure such profound belief?

Why Did They Come?

So we have to raise yet another set of questions. How did they know when to go? How did they know about the Messiah? Did they just sit in their palace one day and say, "You know, life's getting a little slow in Babylon. How about an adventure?" Here is where the story really starts to get interesting, for we have to let our minds flicker back six centuries before their time to find the answer, all the way back to another person keeping watch on his knees.

Return once more to Nebuchadnezzar's victory at Carchemish in 605 B.C., an act fulfilling Old Testament prophecies. Nebuchadnezzar began his looting of Judah by taking the most promising young men into exile to Babylon. Among them was Daniel. In fact, Daniel spent sixty-six years in Persia, many of them under the reign of King Darius, who was himself a Mede—the same tribe as the wise men.

We notice further that Daniel had remarkably similar gifts as the wise men, a fact that made a startling impression on them since it saved their lives. Daniel 2 records a dream of Nebuchadnezzar that the Magi just could not figure out. The apoplectic king was so frustrated he ordered the chief of his guards to execute them all. But during the night God revealed the mystery of the dream to Daniel, who went straightaway to Nebuchadnezzar and traded the interpretation for the lives of the wise men. Immediately Daniel had their gratitude and respect, but he reserved it for another. He told the king: "No wise man . . . can explain to the king the mystery he has asked about, but there is a God in heaven who reveals mysteries" (2:27-28).

It is not simply that God gives interpretations of certain dreams to certain men who claim to be wise. This God, with whom Daniel is acting as intermediary, ordains and directs *all* kingdoms on his earth. As he began the interpretation, Daniel asserted: "The God of heaven has given you dominion and power and might and glory" (Daniel 2:37). And Nebuchadnezzar himself testified to this when his sanity returns: "I, Nebuchadnezzar, raised my eyes toward heaven, and my sanity was restored. Then I praised the Most High" (Daniel 4:34). I can imagine the Magi were awestruck by this God with whom Daniel interceded. Not only did he have power to cast a powerful king into bestial madness, he had the power to restore him to sanity! When Daniel fell to his knees, I wonder if they did also.

But there is a third connection here, linking six hundred years of human history. While the Medes were well-tutored in astronomical signs, Daniel also beheld a vision in the heavens that caused them to pay attention. This time, in chapter 7, Daniel saw a vision of a throne in the heavens that lay far beyond and above any stars; it was the throne room of the "Ancient of Days." Very likely this title for a supreme and eternal ruler was known to the wise men. What was not known to them was the rest of Daniel's vision. In that same throne room Daniel saw one like a "son of man" approach the Ancient of Days.

Now this was odd. Among all the celestial beings, here was a "person," a human like any son of man. Odder still was the fact that it was same name that Jesus often used for himself more than six hundred years later. But there was more. Upon this "person" the Ancient of Days bestowed "authority, glory and sovereign power; all peoples, nations and men of every language worshiped him. His dominion is an everlasting dominion that will not pass away" (Daniel 7:13-14). This was a perfect definition for the Messiah, the anointed One whose sovereign kingdom will last forever.

And so the promises passed into the lore of the Magi. They knew, as they waited and passed along their histories and stories for six hundred years, that a Messiah would be born.

But wait. How did they know *when* to go? In fact they did not. They waited for some sign, hoarding their knowledge and expectations as political insurgents swept across history. None was the Messiah. But we also remember that these wise men were astronomers, ones who looked to the heavens for answers on this earth. And in this way they received their sign.

By the reckoning of most biblical scholars, taking into account inaccuracies in calendar dating, Jesus was probably born four years prior to the era we date as A.D. Shortly before this time the planets Jupiter and Saturn were moving increasingly into conjunction—an astronomical phenomenon that would not have gone unnoticed by the Magi. That is one option; the other is that God prepared a miraculous star that did in fact guide them throughout their journey. This could also be the star of Matthew 2:9. A God who sent his Son to be born of a virgin might very well give a miraculous sign to a people so devoted to finding him.

Whichever the case, can you imagine the conversation in their courts?

"Melchior, this is mad! Insanity, I tell you," said Gaspar.

"Why? This is the sign, isn't it?"

"Sign for what?"

"For the Messiah," said Melchior. "For everything we've waited for all these years!"

"Bah! That's ancient history."

"It's our history. We've waited—"

"And wasted our time waiting."

"Well, Gaspar, if you're not with me, you can stay behind. I'm going."

"I'm with you," said Belteshazzar. "Although it will take enormous work."

"True. Camels, provisions, guides, tents."

"Keep going," said Gaspar, "Grain for the camels. Don't forget water. I've heard the desert gets sort of dry."

"Well, then. The sooner we get started . . . This is the great adventure, brothers. The one we've waited for."

Yes, they had waited. And waited. How does one measure such patience! And now it had run out; it was time to go.

What Did They Find?

We have no historical knowledge for how many Magi actually made the journey. Perhaps more started than finished. Legend has it that three arrived, simply because three gifts are mentioned—gold, frankincense and myrrh. There could have been a dozen or more visitors. The gifts very likely financed Joseph and Mary's flight into Egypt after Herod's edict to kill all the Jewish infants. It is interesting to note that the Magi stop first in Jerusalem. Of course they would. They knew that the Messiah would be born out of Daniel's people, and kings, they believed, always were born in a royal palace in the capital city.

But they went, to the very end, guided the last half dozen miles from Jerusalem to Bethlehem by the prophecy given by Micah approximately seven hundred years earlier. Micah, who also foresaw the exile into Babylon (Micah 4), tells where the Messiah will be born:

"But you, Bethlehem Ephrathah, though you are small among the clans of Judah, out of you will come for me one who will be ruler over Israel, whose origins are from of old, from ancient times" (5:2). Micah goes on to tell of this ruler who will "shepherd his flock in the strength of his LORD, in the majesty of the name of the LORD his God" (5:4). The language is marvelously similar to Daniel's, a fact that would not be lost on these wise men. So they continued. And found the child.

Jesus, who was likely born in the early spring of the year 4 B.C., now lived in a house in Bethlehem with Mary and Joseph. The Magi found them there; they presented their gifts and departed on their long journey home.

Just a coming and going? A brief passage in the annals of history? We know the factual significance—the gifts probably paid for their forced journey to Egypt. But is that all? Or do we begin to measure by some different standards, such as faith and keeping watch? That is a different story than the simple dates and facts that history gives us. That is the important story, for any believer's story is also first and foremost a story of faith and keeping watch.

It has been commonly noted that the wise men, these strangers from the East, represent the Messiah's inclusion of all Gentiles into his kingdom, those fulfilling the prophecy of Daniel 7:14. Truly that is so. All the other guests at the nativity were Jews. Just as truly, it is of minor importance unless we see something of ourselves in the Magi, for he who was to them a king is to us a Savior.

What Do They Mean to Us?

Looking back over the Magi's story, I am struck again by their outrageous passion. They defied all the conventions of their time for one purpose only: to draw near to the side of Christ. The Bible does not tell us if they were befuddled by what they found, whether they rejoiced ecstatically, or whether their hearts were ablaze with glory. No, they simply found whom they were looking for, presented their gifts and headed home.

And that was everything they sought: the One for Whom they were looking. The outrageous passion to find the truth and the heart's home—that drove them across desert wastes—well, it was satisfied. This was the One they had sought. They had left behind homes, treasures and comforts in Babylon—left behind the dead weight of the world to satisfy the heart's passion. They arrived, and found it.

The sense of benediction is soul-bending. It turns on the passion of our own souls and hearts and turns us directly to these questions: What do I seek with all my heart, and soul and strength? What am I willing to leave behind, what distance to travel, what fears to overcome, to bow before the Christ?

The wise men challenge us further, for theirs was a powerful belief. Remember what it was predicated on—the teachings of a foreign prophet named Daniel and a strange light in the heavens. This guides belief? It is preposterous.

Yet they clung to those obscure teachings for six hundred years, waiting the time. Probably we would handle them differently today. Some scholars would get their heads together in a buzz at some conference and talk about myths and pseudomyths and talk until there's nothing left to talk about. Or believe.

But the Magi *believed*. They took this as truth. It may have been intellectually outrageous, but they were wise men, and they did exactly that. Here's the curious implication. If the wise men took it as truth and found it to be true, why shouldn't we? The battle for the Bible today isn't being fought primarily in courts or classrooms; rather, it's being fought in churches and in believers' lives in how we consider it to be true—the Word of God. If it was true for the Magi six hundred years after being spoken, is it any less or more true for us two thousand years after the Magi?

Then there was the matter of the star. The Magi took it as a sign. What would we do with it? Perhaps photograph it? Wait for an analysis on CNN? Talk about it over coffee? The Magi *believed;* they acted. Surely there is another heavenquake coming. The skies will split asunder; the sounds of trumpets will rattle the rocks of the earth, the light of glory will drown out the sun like a used penny. The Son of Man will return. And will we believe?

And finally, the wise men tutor us—uneasy pupils that we are—in faith and patience. When Jesus met the centurion, whose servant he would heal, Jesus exclaimed of this Gentile: "I tell you the truth, I have not found anyone in Israel with such great faith" (Matthew 8:10). The centurion truly believed two things: that Jesus was the Messiah and that he could do all things. The wise men had faith that at the end of the journey they would find the Messiah. They paid homage to him, yet they little knew that he could do all things. They returned to Babylon without benefit of Jesus' ministry, his atonement on the cross or his resurrection. All these we have in addition to the nativity; they nurture our faith and our patience.

In our lives we must—for some of us, often—seek the Christ once again, traveling home to the heart of Jesus to regain living contact. It seems sometimes a journey we make endlessly, over and over. Yet it is a journey which in itself nurtures our faith. At the close of his study *The Problem of Pain* (Macmillan, 1962), C. S. Lewis observes: "It is safe to tell the pure in heart that they shall see God, for only the pure in heart want to" (p. 145). Sometimes, however, our faith has been beaten into the ground, like ruts on a hard, clay road, and we just can't find a way to go. Or it may be that our own hearts appear to us sullied and impure. So we keep traveling to Bethlehem, keeping faith that the one whom we seek is eager to greet us when we arrive. So much patience is required in the journey. Indeed, some of us will not feel the greeting until the angels lovingly usher us into the eternal throne room of the Messiah. But then we can look up to see, not the Child of Bethlehem, but the Lord of lords in his eternal palace.

For Further Study

Read Matthew 2; Hebrews 10:5-10

1. It is often said that the Magi represent all future Gentiles coming to know Jesus. How does the Hebrews 10 passage affirm this? Bear in mind that the Magi knew nothing about Jewish law and sacred rituals; they came only with what gifts they had.

2. Mary and Joseph were so poor they could hardly afford the most meager temple sacrifice. Now they had to flee to Egypt. In the Matthew account of the coming of the Magi, how can we see God's providential hand at work?

3. Think of ways your spiritual pilgrimage may be like the Magi's. What frustrations or uncertainties might be the same? What joys?

4. One of the most commonly discussed topics in reference to the Magi is wisdom. What did being wise mean specifically for them, that is, in their appointed role in Babylon? In what other ways might the term *wise* apply to them and to us?

5. The Magi challenge us to discover the true passions in our life—those things that really matter and for which we are willing to devote our whole lives. What is the difference between wisdom as knowledge and wisdom as a passion?

Prayer

This story, Lord, fills me with fear and trembling. It is that powerful, and somehow I have overlooked it before. Perhaps because I didn't dare confront its truth. I have to measure everything in my life according to my passion for you. I have to let my faith in you rock me like a holy fire, burning out anything that would turn me from you, turning me wholly toward you. And I realize I am not able to do that on my own. On my own I stand convicted—unworthy. I pray for the power of your Holy Spirit to cleanse, renew and direct me. Amen.

13

The Miracle of Faithfulness
MARY MAGDALENE

*T*HE WOMAN SLIPPED ACROSS THE WATCHFUL ROOM, A ROOM SHE didn't belong in. This was a proper house, where formality governed and etiquette was forever observed.

Of course she slipped in unannounced, for her life had been a long impropriety. She was a sinful woman, and now had the audacity to enter a Pharisee's house. Fearful, she stood there. Trembling, she edged in through the people gathered around, clutching something precious to her breast.

Why on earth would she dare the despite of the haughty? Why crash this party in the Pharisee's house? Why? Because she had heard Jesus was a dinner guest there.

For the same reason that a woman who had an issue of blood burst through the crowd to touch the hem of Jesus' garment, this woman came. For the same reason that the leper fell to his knees at Jesus' feet on the dusty roadside, this woman came. For the same reason that the centurion sought Jesus to heal his servant, this woman came.

She came because she loved him, and because he could return love even to a sinful woman.

If Jesus is in the room, it is a safe place. Fear can be left at the door.

Her eyes raked the room looking for him. There. At the long table. He reclined among the other guests, facing the table, bare feet stretched out behind him.

Bravely she made her way around the table, standing behind him. And now . . . maybe she feared rejection. The expensive perfume in the alabaster cruse seemed so cheap now. But it had cost so much. What if he laughed at her! No. He wouldn't.

The tension rose. She trembled. They were discussing something she didn't understand. Maybe they thought she was just the serving girl.

Frantically she ripped at the seal on the long-necked bottle. The light wasn't good; she couldn't see where the seal adjoined the white face of the bottle. What if they saw? And how was she to reach over and anoint his head? Too many bodies—too close together.

Suddenly she began weeping. Tears like sheets rolled down her cheeks. Her shoulders shook. But she vowed not to cry aloud. Alone! She had always been alone. It was her curse. Those who came to her came to leave her. A sinful woman. Miraculously she found her fingernails under the edge of the seal. She ripped it off and hurled it away.

She was looking down, about to step between the prone bodies, when she saw the moisture of her tears on Jesus' feet. Did he feel it? His feet were dusty. And again her tears fell, but softly now, and safely—as if each were caught in a hand of love. Tears fell, but she smiled as she knelt.

As she leaned forward she pulled the piece of linen that bound her long dark hair and it fell out like a flight of ravens. The talk stopped suddenly. She felt every eye on her, heard the collective insuck of breath as she took the wings of her raven hair and gently, oh, so gently, dried the gift of tears, her anointing oil. The dust of the road clung to his ankles; she massaged them clean, her hair now damp and gritty.

And then she smiled—no, giggled out loud—for she still held in her hand the alabaster bottle, gleaming softly in the light of the oil lamps, in her hand. She kneeled, and the group of men hushed. Tenderly she bent her head, and gently she kissed those feet. She held each, and it was like holding love in her hands. Then she tilted the alabaster cruse and let the rich perfume, in a slow, delicate stream, flow over Jesus' feet.

The Pharisee had had enough. Yes, Jesus was a guest in his house, but it was *his* house. To himself the Pharisee muttered, "She's a sinner."

Jesus heard the words, however covertly spoken. He came to the defense of the one who loved him, the one he loved. Yes, as the Pharisee said, she was a sinner. But Jesus said, "I tell you, her many sins have been forgiven—for she loved much" (Luke 7:47). Then, as if to make it official, Jesus turned to the woman behind him and said, "Your sins are forgiven." And as she rose to leave, Jesus added, "Your faith has saved you; go in peace" (7:50).

Jesus' benediction on this woman is a soul-saver: a forgiveness of sins, an assurance of faith, and a benediction of peace. It is everything she longed for—and everything we long for. If she entered Jesus' presence tremulously, her sins as evident as a badge, well-known to everyone, one wonders how she left. With a benediction like that! Go in peace; your sins are forgiven. Your faith has saved you. We only know how she left his presence by the way we leave, for each of us has to come, baring the heart of sin, seeking forgiveness, believing by faith that it will be granted. Do we leave skipping and dancing? Songs on our lips? Renewal in our hearts? Oh, there is much to say about this woman, for she says so much about us.

The only trouble is, we don't even know her name. She was *known* by Jesus; that suffices. Popular belief has identified this woman as Mary Magdalene—the faithful one. And perhaps she was, but there is no biblical evidence to support that conclusion. We do know that, like this unnamed woman, Mary Magdalene exemplifies faithfulness, clinging against all odds to what she believed. Mary, too, is a paragon for us in steadfastly keeping watch, of being faithful even in the darkness to the light everlasting. Here is the rest of what we know about Mary.

Mary Delivered

She is first mentioned, almost casually, in Luke 8 as one of several women in the party including the twelve disciples who accompanied Jesus. Luke distinguishes these women as those "who had been cured of evil spirits and diseases" (v. 2). The first listed among these women, at least several of whom were "helping to support [Jesus and his disciples] out of their own means" (v. 3), was Mary Magdalene.

Two items distinguish her in the brief identification. First, she is called Magdalene because her home town was Magdala, a town on the west shore of the Sea of Galilee, just south of Capernaum. Although little is known of this inconsequential town in Jesus' day, it is likely that after Jesus' miracle of feeding the crowds he crossed over into this area.

The second distinguishing trait in this brief note by Luke is that it was this Mary "from whom seven demons had come out" (Luke 8:2). Perhaps this notice and the close proximity to Luke 6 have led some people to identify Mary with the sinful woman of that chapter. But that need not be the case.

The Gospels make fairly frequent reference to demons, signifying by that word spiritual beings hostile to God and under the direction of Satan. The effects of their presence in humans were varied—from dumbness, to seizures, to abandonment in waste places. Since the demons were under the authority of Satan, they had very substantial power over humans—but not over the Lord of heaven and earth. The earliest phases of Jesus' ministry were marked by his spiritual authority over these cunning beings; in fact, they were some of the first beings publicly to recognize who Jesus was. Well they should; Jesus was their absolute spiritual master.

Mark 1 (also Luke 4) recounts the story of Jesus healing the demon-possessed man in the synagogue. It is the demon who speaks to Jesus: "What do you want with us, Jesus of Nazareth? Have you come to destroy us? I know who you are—the Holy One of God" (Mark 1:24). With exceptional clarity and force the true nature of Jesus, Lord of all spiritual beings, is revealed. How it must have chilled Jesus to the core, then, when the theologians came down from Jerusalem to confront him. They thought they had put everything in logical order, finding a neat, little rational category to put Jesus in: "He is possessed by Beelzebub! By the prince of demons he is driving out demons" (Mark 3:22). I don't have any more inclination toward violence than any other man I know, but I do believe I would have been hard-pressed not to explode at those pompous bigwigs with their twisted logic. Jesus, however, is a good deal calmer, although one can certainly sense the irritation in his words as he exposed the folly of their thinking.

The key pattern here is that demonic activity was widely evident during the time of Jesus, that Jesus engaged in spiritual combat with the demons, and that his deliverance of wounded humans from the grip of evil was a stunning miracle. So it was that Mary Magdalene, who had once been devastated by seven demons, was now delivered and entered into grateful service to the Lord who had delivered her. She saw things logically, through the eyes of faith: If this man cast out demons from me, delivering me from evil, then he has authority over evil. And authority over me as I choose to follow him. I will walk where he walks; I will work to support him rather than myself; I will make him Lord of my life because I trust him entirely to do the very best with my life.

Every true believer since has walked in the way of Mary Magdalene, echoing her words.

Mary's Bold Faithfulness

Mary's example in faithful watchkeeping extends further than this mere, but essential, support of Jesus' ministry. In fact, it extends to his death. And his resurrection.

Reflect for a moment on those faithful ones keeping watch in Old Testament times. Isaiah, Amos, Daniel, Esther. What would their lives have been like had they lived right at the time of Jesus? Or David, way back in a thousand-year lineage? But Mary *was* there! And her calling, at that time and place where she lived, was no different than the others. She was called to be faithful. To keep watch.

So many fell away in those last desperate days. They scattered in fear and hid.

But not the women—these brave, beautifully bold women. Many women "had come up with him to Jerusalem," and among them were "Mary Magdalene, Mary the mother of James the younger and of Joses, and Salome" (Mark 15:40-41). They climbed the rugged road to Golgotha. They stayed on its wind-bitten slopes as the sky darkened and the earth shook. They fixed their eyes on the cross even when the sky turned black and they wept in each other's arms. How powerful their loyalty; how fierce their tenderness.

They saw the Savior die. They went home weeping.

But here's what Mary did.

Along with the mother of Joses, Mary kept watch, following to see exactly where Jesus' body was laid. On seeing the entombment, they went home to prepare additional spices and perfumes to wrap Christ's body in. Still their Lord, even in death.

They had only one problem. The next day was the Sabbath. They had to wait until it was over before they could properly care for their Lord.

But Mary Magdalene could hardly wait. The sun was just shooting its first shocking light over the eastern sky when she arrived with a few of the other women at the tomb. And found it empty. The stone had been rolled away from its entrance. Then, like the light of the rising sun itself, an angel appeared to announce the resurrection of their Lord.

The first ones at the tomb, the faithful ones, were the first also to hear the great news.

But there is still more to the story of faithful Mary. As the Gospel of John tells the story, Mary alone remained by the tomb. Another man appeared to her, this time to comfort her. "Mary," he said. And she turned and said—did she whisper, half fearful of the answer?— "Rabboni." Whereupon Jesus charges her to bring the good news of his resurrection to the others.

There are, of course, variations in the differing narratives of the resurrection. In the case of Mary Magdalene, however, the evidence of her faithfulness is irrefutable. Mary was the faithful one, always there at Jesus' side during the dusty days of his earthly ministry. She supported him with an unflinching loyalty, even on the lonely march to Golgotha. But the larger testimony is that her faithfulness is requited; the resurrected Christ came to her—first to her—to bless her fidelity.

So much in my own life works to skew the course of faithfulness. At times I have strayed far too far from the side of Jesus. There have been moments when I have been plunged into a psychological bleakness as thick as the black sky over Golgotha. Yet I take courage from Mary, with the seemingly unswerving heart. For even at my farthest remove from Jesus' side, I have yearned like a lonely pilgrim for a closer walk. And have found it. For while my faithfulness is flawed, his is perfect. He awaits me with a blessing also.

In one of her powerful poems inspired by the Gospels, this one entitled *A Better Resurrection,* Christina Georgina Rossetti captures perfectly this feeling I am writing about. I quote the last two stanzas of the poem:

My life is like a faded leaf,
My harvest dwindled to a husk:
Truly my life is void and brief
   And tedious in the barren dusk;
My life is like a frozen thing,
   No bud nor greenness can I see;
Yet rise it shall—the sap of Spring;
   O Jesus, rise in me.

My life is like a broken bowl,
   A broken bowl that cannot hold
One drop of water for my soul
   Or cordial in the searching cold;
Cast in the fire the perished thing;

Melt and remould it, till it be
A royal cup for Him, my King:
O Jesus, drink of me.

The story of Mary Magdalene is not just about a woman healed at the master's touch, however miraculous that may be. Nor is it just about her unswerving faithfulness, however laudable that may be. Rather, her life is sort of a parable for what happens in me and countless other believers. When "life is like a faded leaf," it is dry and brittle. The sharp little edges needle into you, and they hurt. Life has gone gray, faded from all color. But—and it is a huge assertion—even though I can't see any green, I believe that "yet rise it shall—the sap of Spring." Because of Christ "rising" in me.

Some of us also know times when life is very much like a broken bowl. The shards lie sprawled across the kitchen floor and we despair of ever putting it back together. We feel exactly as if we should be swept up and tossed out with the garbage. It is a useless thing, this life, this broken bowl. It can't hold a drop of water. But—and again the assertion makes all the difference in life and in death—the potter can take me into his house. He can melt and remold this life "till it be / A royal cup for Him, my King." So we offer our lives to him, even when the offering doesn't appear to be worth much to us. Offer it, and plead, "O Jesus, drink of me."

The wonder of Mary Magdalene's faithful watchkeeping is the faithfulness of Jesus to Mary Magdalene. Can you imagine this: of all people, he chose to appear as a risen Savior to her first. But, you see, that faithfulness does not end there. It awaits each of us, with whatever offerings of our lives we are able to bring.

For Further Study

Read Luke 8:1-2; John 20:11-18

1. Mary was a woman delivered by Jesus from the bondage of seven demons. How did she use her freedom?

2. On the first day of the week Mary arrived at the tomb "while it was still

dark." What does this tell us about her?

3. The faithfulness of the women who followed Jesus, as this chapter makes clear, was truly astonishing. We would do well to measure our own faithfulness according to theirs. What lessons can we learn from John 20 about faithfully keeping watch for the Savior?

4. Most important in John 20 is that the Savior is faithful to us. How is this so? How did Jesus fulfill promises he made earlier in his life?

5. Perhaps the most specific application of faithfulness occurs at the end of John 20. Read verses 29-31 and reflect on how they apply to us specifically and individually.

Prayer

Mary saw the glory of the risen Lord. What a morning that was, when all her faithfulness was rewarded a millionfold. But I thank you, Jesus, for this story also confirms the certain answers for my own watchkeeping. May you find me faithful, ready to greet the risen Lord. Amen.

14

Saints & Sinners
THE DISCIPLES

*M*ISS SELINA HICKS DIRECTED OUR THIRD-GRADE SUNDAY-SCHOOL class with a voice like a rasp and a set of pale blue eyes that seemed chiseled out of a block of ice. I was sorely tempted to skip third-grade Sunday school; all the perils to my soul could not hold a candle to the legendary wrath of Miss Hicks.

Out of range—*far* out of range—of her hearing we had a mean-spirited and innovative set of nicknames for her: Missicks. Mesick. Helena Sick, Miss Hix and the like. Strange how easily I can remember what I should forget. And yet, when I remember Miss Hicks honestly, I can't recall one minute during that long year when she demonstrated any overt meanness, anger or bitterness. Maybe we just didn't like the sound of her voice or the set of her eyes; third-grade boys can be like that. More likely, the legend that preceded Miss Hicks was more formidable than reality itself.

During that year with Miss Hicks came my introduction to the disciples. That is, in the curriculum we followed, we had to memorize all the disciples' names. This was a small task to anyone whose memory cells in the brain functioned smoothly; that is, normally. Mine at that age functioned more like my father's old V8 Ford Fairlane—it was questionable whether it would run at all, and, if it did, whether it would get us anywhere near our destination. But there was one larger incentive for me. If the dutiful third-grader completed this simple (for others) task, he or she was awarded a stunning little white Bible with gilt-edged leaves. It was a thing to make a boy swear off worldly amusements, to devote himself to the task of memorization. My memory cells sweated with the effort. In the latter stages I'm convinced there were tiny little ruptures as one cell after the other caved in under the pressure.

When the great day came, I could tell the visiting elders in a snap that Alphaeus had a son named James. I thought James might be a disciple, but I really liked the name Alphaeus. Now there's a true disciple's name. It sounded like Hector, or Achilles, the stories I was devouring in simplified versions. I could have told them a lot about Priam's ruined throne or fierce Lycurgus. I remembered Simon because he was from Canaan, and somehow that seemed a truly remarkable place to originate. But from there on I was firing on seven cylinders of an overheated engine, then six, and so on. I got maybe six or eight of the names out altogether. Could I help it that my head was stuffed with quirky, useless information? Apparently the elders thought not, or they thought I had made my best use of a severely restricted talent. They gave me a little white Bible anyway. And from that time I developed a cordial, but distant relationship with the disciples that lasted many years.

For as I was growing up, and studying the Bible more as God's revelation and less as a set of puzzles and memory words, it seemed sufficient to tuck the disciples off into a corner marked "God's Heroes. Saints. Do Not Disturb." And, truly, for years following, when their famous and fabled names would trip off the lips of friends or my own, that was my response. Here are the heroes, who braved the threat of persecution to serve their Messiah. They drove out demons, healed the sick, battled sin. Far more worthy than any storybook fictional heroes. And here are the saints, who walked in the Messiah's footsteps enduring hunger, the bitterness of Judean weather, the hostility of humans—knowing that great is their reward in heaven.

Oh, to be like them.

Then, I became aware of another attitude toward the disciples. It began first with intensifying efforts during the 1980s at some liberal divinity schools to "demythologize" the Bible, to explain in concrete, scientific and often naturalistic form what heretofore had been shrouded in the mystery of God's omniscience. One example of this is the effort to explain all miracles solely in terms of natural forces. As this practice gained intellectual momentum during the 1980s, it began to question all things sacred, including of course the authenticity of passages of Scripture itself. These scholars began to wonder what Jesus really said, and if he said it, what did he mean by it?

With the same supercilious scorn they turned their attention to the disciples. They were now pictured as a collection of freaks, a rogue's gallery of misfits who, like their perplexed leader, couldn't quite make it in society.

The scorn infected some preaching in mainline churches also. Peter, the Son of Thunder, became a belligerent anarchist. John, well, he was at least a potential homosexual. And Thomas? He was the first-century equivalent of the liberal scholar, requiring some sort of tangible proof from a theological nightmare. He was with Jesus from the start, their argument goes, so if even Jesus' own disciples couldn't figure out his plan, how much less can we?

And congregations responded, "Oh, we're glad we're not like them."

Unfortunately, we are very much like them—for better or for worse, struggling toward sainthood in a bewildering world.

I have two propositions I want to explore in this chapter: first, that Jesus' band of disciples—excluding Judas but including his replacement, Matthias—were saints; and, second, that all Jesus' children—including us in the years since—are also saints.

Part of the argument here, albeit a rather small one, is linguistic.

The word *hagios,* used in the New Testament, is of relatively uncertain derivation, and so serves several meanings. It may derive from a word meaning "separation" or "to be cut off," often signifying a sense of being separated for divine service. Another form of it bears the meaning of "pure"; still another, of "beloved." What all these have in common is a loving relationship with God, and, we might add, one that so defines the person that he or she stands apart from the world in spiritual matters. It may apply to persons "consecrated" to a certain office, like the Old Testament Levitical priests, or still again to believers in general who love God and seek to serve him.

That last clause may be the troubling one, for believers in the first-century church, including the disciples, were generally referred to as "saints." Thus, Paul writes to the Romans, "To all in Rome who are loved by God and called to be saints" (1:7). But we detect a peculiarity there: "*called* to be saints." The word suggests a process that believers are working on, not a state instantaneously or miraculously attained. Salutations of Paul in other letters follow a similar pattern. Sainthood, then, seems to be part of our Christian living— our loving relationship with God—enacted in this world. Interestingly, one of several deviations in the salutation occurs in Paul's warm letter to the Ephesians: "To the saints in Ephesus, the faithful in Christ Jesus." Several other epistles bear this more emphatic, affirming salutation, which strongly encourages people doing their best to walk in the way of the Lord in this life now.

There is some tension or division here then. Is sainthood something reserved for heaven? Or is it something required of believers now?

Although the term was used commonly for believers during the first century, that use waned during the next century. Much later it was reinstated by the church to recognize persons whose lives were so exemplary, so very nearly perfect, that they merited canonization for all common believers to follow. Once again, like some bizarre yo-yo, sainthood spirals from common believer to beatified human. And it has left modern believers mightily confused. Ask a person if she's a saint and, if she's thinking of the first-century church, she can rightly respond yes. Should she be thinking of those pillars of faith beatified by an act of the church, she can rightly respond no.

One final curve in the argument, before we arrive at conclusions, comes into play. The doctrine of the Fall, central to our understanding of sin and need for grace, holds that "all have sinned and fall short of the glory of God" (Romans 3:23). Isaiah put it like this: "All our righteous acts are like filthy rags" (64:6), perhaps a very clever reference to Job who said, "I put on righteousness as my clothing" (29:14). We *cannot help sinning* in our human condition. Does that mean that sainthood is reserved for us only in heaven, where, as an old hymn has it, "saints in glory stand?" There is a difficulty even with the hymn, for that will be our resurrected body, when we are in a state when we *cannot sin.* If there is no separation from evil and temptation, but only and always a unity with Christ, can we properly speak of sainthood?

Thinking about sainthood takes us down a crooked, winding road. But I think it is worthwhile. It will tell us some things about the disciples, about first-century believers, even about ourselves.

Certainly the disciples were no saints in the sense of perfection of behavior, nor in their thorough separation from the world. Indeed, one might well wonder why they are even included in this collection of persons keeping watch for the Messiah. They were right with him all the time, and Jesus still had to make his person explicit: "If you really knew me, you would know my father as well. From now on, you do know him and have seen him" (John 14:7). Nor did they keep watch very well. They were the eyewitnesses, but they averted their eyes. The night before his arrest Jesus retreated with his disciples to pray. Oh, he knew what was coming. And he prayed mightily. But the disciples? They fell asleep. To Peter, Jesus spoke these haunting words: "Could you not keep watch for one hour? Watch and pray so you will not fall into temptation" (Mark 14:37-38).

The issue here is not that we have to redefine the disciples to fit some more human model. There is no need for that; they evidenced with a sobering reality the shortcomings—psychological, spiritual and physical—of any one of us. What is necessary is to look to them and gain heart. Let's take sainthood out of the slice of holy canonization and put it back in the daily living of believers where it belongs. Sainthood is the way of Christian living: struggling daily against sin and putting God over the temptation. I would go so far as to call sainthood the spiritual warfare in which each of us engages.

And it is also a rhythm of living, devotion to our calling, lovingkindness even to the unlovely.

I have read Graham Greene's *The Power and the Glory* (Penguin, 1940, rpt. 1977) at least half a dozen times. It rewards me each time I come back to it. Not because the author was a particularly spiritual man; he was not. Nor because the plot is so startling or original; for it isn't. Nor even for the particular power of its prose; it is strong but hardly dazzling. What draws me back and back is the little scarecrow figure of the main character, the Whiskey Priest. He is at once so despicable I want to loathe him, and also so heroic I want to bow to receive his blessing. He is a saint who is certain he isn't one; indeed, a list of his misdeeds seems to exclude him from any consideration.

Following a Marxist revolution in a fictional Central American country, the new government bans the two greatest evils to the people: alcohol and religion. Both turn a person *from* reality; both are destructive of the person. The Whiskey Priest has both great evils, and he has been on the run, an outlaw, for years. In fact, as the story begins we see his shabby little figure waiting for a chance to escape aboard a riverboat, but a child comes and calls for his services to a presumably dying person, and the Whiskey Priest bows his shoulders and follows the indelible and undeniable calling of his soul.

His adversary is a steely lieutenant of the new order who has resolved to destroy everything if he cannot catch the priest. For him, abject vacancy is better than what he sees as the corrupt perversity of religion. He lives for the people—only the people. In his view, religion enslaves people under a yoke of abusive power and deceptive ritual. The lieutenant, who is depicted often as a sort of priest of his new world order, reflects on the outrage of religion: "It infuriated him to think that there were still people in the state who believed in a loving and merciful God. . . . What he had experienced was vacancy— a complete certainty in the evidences of a dying, cooling world, of human beings who had evolved from animals for no purpose at all" (pp. 24-25). So he becomes the crusader, the priest, of the new, antireligious world order.

And meanwhile, the alcoholic priest of God slips from one little village to another, begging some food, unable to deny the peoples' petitions for his religious acts. And always, always, he accedes to them. Unwillingly, to be sure, but he cannot help it. This is what he is, despite the mountain of flaws he drags on his back: he is a priest of God.

And there lies the power of *The Power and the Glory,* for it touches the core of any and every believer who, however beset by sin or heartache in this world, nonetheless follows the call of God. The really big challenge is not whether we are willing to die for Christ, for such commonly constitutes our idea of sainthood. No, the really big challenge is whether we are willing to live for Christ, for this constitutes the sainthood of any believer. Daily we saints struggle against sin, desperately trying to put God before the temptation. And time after time we have to come crawling back to the throne of grace, pleading, "Father, forgive me."

Late in the book the Whiskey Priest is caught, brought to a cell, and scheduled for execution. To say just *how* this happens would give away the drama of the plot. But one key moment stands out. He recalls the question of an Indian child, "What is God like?" He reflects on the only correct answer on this earth: "At the centre of his own faith there always stood the convincing mystery—that we are made in God's image" (p. 101). We, then, project God forth for others, such as the wondering little boy. Surely we fail, but we strive to fit the image.

At the end, the Whiskey Priest is mindful only of how badly he has failed that task. Unable to find a confessor who will come to his cell in the now vacant and godless state, he begins to confess himself and is staggered by the accumulation of his own sin. With twists of irony, his confession ends: "He felt only an immense disappointment because he had to go to God empty-handed, with nothing done at all. It seemed to him, at that moment, that it would have been quite easy to have been a saint. It would only have needed a little self-restraint and a little courage" (p. 210). And so he is executed, lamenting the littleness of his life.

But that little life of sainthood—a simultaneous struggle to serve God and fight sin—leaves its seeds of new life for others. As the swaggering and polished lieutenant patrols the God-free streets of his town, one of the little boys who witnessed the execution spits in his direction: "A little blob of spittle lay on the revolver-butt."

The deeds of saints tend to live on. This is not necessarily because of their heroism, either for Jesus' disciples, or the Whiskey Priest, or even for ourselves. It is because in the struggle against sin, one is faithful. It is often less the sin that matters than the fidelity that endures. Saints—the disciples, the Whiskey Priest, or even us—are like those people who join Saint Paul in proclaiming: "For I am convinced that neither death nor life, neither angels nor demons, neither the present nor the future, nor any powers, neither height nor depth, nor anything else in all creation, will be able to separate us from the love of God that is in Christ Jesus our Lord" (Romans 8:38-39). Our sainthood doesn't depend on what we do; rather on what Jesus has done.

Take the argument back full circle to Jesus' disciples. Were they God's heroes, true saints ushering in and establishing the church of Jesus Christ? Of course. Absolutely. What a task it was too, and let's not forget that several died in this cause. Or, were they all too human to be saints—crude, rough-mannered, given to flights of temper rather than fancy? Yes, that too. But still saints. Despite any traits of character or manner, they were uniquely gifted by God to do his kingdom work.

All except one, of course. For there was one disciple who irretrievably spent his sainthood. He didn't just turn against the church, he turned on the Savior. While the others kept poor watch indeed—all too human in the late night—this one kept too sharp a watch. He was looking out for himself before anything else. When he found it—this hidden self—and saw how very cheap and shabby it was (What? Thirty pieces of silver! That's all?) there was only one thing left for him: despair. No, this was no saint, this Judas Iscariot.

Like these disciple saints of old, we will find our watch keeping forever flawed; sometimes we won't know grace even when it stands an arm's length away. But also like them, we will not know despair. Finally, the disciples sought the heavenly vision, the celestial prize. While Judas flung himself headlong into the darkness of the potter's field, the disciples learned how to keep better watch. They learned how to bring God's kingdom about. And they also kept watch for the light of glory to guide their way. Jesus said, "And surely I will be with you always, to the very end of the age" (Matthew 28:20). What and whom they sought was fast among them.

So what do we make of the disciples? Befuddled humans, often bewildered in their divine calling? Certainly. One can hardly deny that; the evidence is too thick. What else, saints? Yes. I add that, for despite their human weakness they desperately sought to serve, and often succeeded in serving, the God who called them. Heroes? In their own quirky way, yes. Especially if you let a hero fail now and then.

And now the big question: Are they like us? Or we like them? At once saints and sinners, we are their spiritual descendants as we attempt to follow the same light—changeless and eternal—that they did.

For Further Study

Read Luke 6:12-16

1. In the Luke passage (the disciples are also listed in Mark 3:13-19 and Matthew 10:2-4) it appears that Jesus selected his "inner circle" of twelve men from a much larger number of followers generally called disciples. Why do you think Jesus chose these twelve? Are there special things about them,

or is it the working of the Holy Spirit through them?

2. How would you define *saint*? Would it bother you if someone called you a saint? What would your reaction be?

3. In our own state we are sinful. Read 1 John 4:13-21. How does it explain that even though we are sinful, we can still be saints? Does it give some insight into what happened to Judas?

4. This chapter defines our personal sainthood as "a rhythm of living, a devotion to our calling, a lovingkindness even to the unlovely." Do you find this definition personally helpful? What might you want to add for yourself?

5. A second key message in this chapter is that "our sainthood doesn't depend on what we do; rather on what Jesus has done." How does this tie together the problem of being both saint and sinner? It is an issue each one of us has to face squarely on individual terms: What has Jesus done for me so that I merit sainthood? What am I required, then, to do in response?

Prayer

Trying to make it on my own, Lord, I feel the words of that old song like a present reality. I am tired. I am worn. I am carrying a sack of "trying to do things my way," and it has me bent to my knees. It is full of my sins—I won't call them "mistakes" anymore—and they are sharp and heavy. I pray to you to reach down. Show me where to dump it out or lift it off my back. I can't do it on my own, Lord, but I do want to do it. Amen.

15

Blinded by the Light
TWO MEN

*T*HERE IS A MAN WHO APPEARS ONLY IN THE GOSPEL OF JOHN, remarkably absent from the other Gospels. To be sure, we have few details about his past, his lineage, even his place of birth—those common identification cards of biblical people. He is simply a blind man by the side of the road. He had been blind since birth, and he was begging to make a living in a dark world.

Certainly we can make a few conjectures about him. He was probably begging somewhere in the lower city of Jerusalem, not too far from the temple where, shortly before, the mob had tried to stone Jesus for identifying himself as the "I am." After healing this blind man, Jesus bade him wash in the pool of *Siloam,* an old, rock-cut pool at the southern edge of the city. The name Siloam means "sent"; appropriately, since the One sent by God sends the blind beggar there. This was not the elite section of Jerusalem. In the eyes of the world, these were not special characters playing out a drama of large spiritual significance. But the world was wrong, for this passing scene on the back street of Jerusalem, with a backdrop of tawdry houses wilting under the blazing sun, was filled with implications that continue to speak loudly in our ears today. Unless, of course, we choose to avoid the "lower sections." Unless, of course, we stay with the healthy and whole in the temple. But that is not the way Jesus went.

The blind beggar of John 9 was keeping watch, but not for the Messiah. He sat apart from any other character in this book. How could he keep watch? He was apart from everything except the dusty little section of the road where he begged. He kept watch for a few coins to stay alive. He measured life in copper inches, a few pennies for another day's life. He was blind. That was all of it—useless in society, forgotten by others.

But Jesus sees—always—what others fail to see. And he didn't pass the blind man by.

His disciples were ready to. For them, having just observed the argumentative fireworks in the temple, the blind man was an object lesson for discussion. Mercy, they were themselves a bit like the Pharisees, aloofly discussing a person as if he were a category in some logical proposition. "Who sinned," they asked Jesus, "this man or his parents that he was *born* blind?" (John 9:2). It was an old chestnut of a discussion question in Jesus' day, especially since some rabbis argued that even a child in the womb could be polluted by sin, or could inherit the punishment for the sins of their parents. This is the sort of thing a Messiah should know and offer an answer to. For a Messiah had all the answers, right? The disciples must have been rubbing their hands in excitement.

The Law and the Lord

Very likely this is the way the disciples thought as they raised their theological/philosophical question to Jesus. What they should have thought was quite different. They had the background; they didn't know how to apply it to the moment.

The disciples knew that the Old Testament prophets thought of the Messiah as a king and that they also thought of him as one who opens the eyes of the blind to spiritual truth. Isaiah frequently used this metaphor, and Jesus quoted this prophet on numerous occasions. In Isaiah 29:18 the prophet declares, "Out of gloom and darkness the eyes of the blind will see." Again, in 35:5, Isaiah says that "then will the eyes of the blind be opened and the ears of the deaf unstopped."

Apart from the testimony of the prophets, the disciples had somehow missed Jesus' own teaching about himself. One wonders, *When will they ever learn?* Only a short time before, the Jews, working like some high-paid courtroom lawyers, tried to corner Jesus with argument. Jesus testified with deeds and the authority from his Father in heaven. The premise for his argument was simple: "I am the light of the world. Whoever follows me will never walk in darkness, but will have the light of life" (John 8:12). Who needs the light but those blind to their sin? Freedom, Jesus goes on to explain, lies in the Son himself (8:36), and it is not only a freedom from the darkness and blindness of this world, but also from the everlasting darkness of death (8:51).

This frames the backdrop for Jesus' response to his disciples. It's as if he is saying, "You still don't get it. You're thinking in terms of the law when the life-bringer is at your side." So he answers his disciples, "Neither this man nor his parents sinned, but this happened so that the work of God might be displayed in his life" (John 9:3). Borrowing his earlier analogy, he adds, "While I am in the world, I am the light of the world" (v. 5). Jesus' concern isn't to argue but to act. To demonstrate his power of the light over darkness, he mixes some spit with clay from the ground, anoints the man's eyes with it, and sends him to the pool of Siloam, from which he emerges seeing clearly. He sees the light that escaped the others.

A splendid moment of grace. A light shone in one man's darkness.

Grace and the Legalists

Then the trouble started. The Pharisees wanted to seal grace up in a little wooden box called the law, doling it out according to their standards. This flow of grace, this living water that washes blindness from a man's eyes—this they wanted to quell. It was very dangerous to their order.

It started innocently enough. The man's neighbors, understandably, asked him what happened. Not an unusual response. I'd be curious too. But the man's response was another matter: "The man they call Jesus made some mud and put it on my eyes" (John 9:11). And they asked, "Where is this man?" They wanted to know more; they wanted to see Jesus.

The Pharisees, catching the buzz of gossip like airmail, called the man to them. They had a trick up their sleeve called the law, for, we discover, the day on which Jesus healed the man was the Sabbath. They turned their narrow heads to each other, gripped in contention: Jesus can't be from God if he broke the Sabbath! But he healed the man!

Unable to reach a settlement, the Pharisees dragged the blind man back to his parents, who identified him as their son. But they tell the Pharisees to talk to him directly: "He is of age; he will speak for himself" (John 9:21). They were looking out for themselves, for the word was out that anyone who claimed Jesus was the Messiah would be tossed out of the synagogue. Excommunicated.

So the Pharisees turned back to the man who had been blind. "Give glory to God and tell the truth," they told him. "Jesus is a sinner." The man ignored the argument about sin entirely—a neat, tidy lesson for the disciples too. They had also tried to categorize the blind man according to sin. But Jesus didn't do that. He liberated from sin. The blind man had experienced the hand of freedom with the touch on his eyes. He explained, "Whether he is a sinner or not, I don't know. One thing I do know. I was blind but now I see!" (John 9:25).

Such is the explanation of all who have come to Jesus for liberation. All those who murmur or shout, "All I know is that I met this man called Jesus, and now I can see," stand with the blind man in his joyful liberation. What a contrast to the Pharisees and even Jesus' own disciples, slugging it out with each other in intellectual argument. And what an irony also, for they excommunicated the man from the house of law—the synagogue, "They threw him out" (John 9:34).

Thrown out, however, the blind man again lands at Jesus' feet (as if the Master had just been waiting for him), where he can acknowledge and worship the true God.

One of my favorite short stories is an often hilarious piece by Philip Roth called "Conversion of the Jews." A young boy named Ozzie Freedman gets in a bitter argument with his rabbi on whether God can do all things, even cause a virgin birth. Ozzie brings the argument home to his mother who cuts it off with a slap across his face. When he starts in again with the rabbi, Ozzie gets hit in the nose (perhaps accidentally) and storms out of the room with his nose bleeding. But where to run?

In a panic Ozzie follows a set of steps and arrives at the roof of the school. In desperation he shouts out that if they pursue him, he'll jump. He races from one end of the roof to the other, rather enjoying the circus act he has engineered as students, passersby and eventually the fire department gather on the lawn below to watch him. Ozzie, Roth writes, "felt Peace, and he felt Power." Why? Simply because for the first time in his life he has possessed and exercised some control in his own life, tasting freedom behind the rules like a delicious meringue.

But dusk is falling. His mother arrives. And the end to his antics is near. So in one grand, final gesture, Ozzie commands everyone to kneel down and confess that God can do anything—even a virgin birth. As the crowd dutifully kneels, Ozzie shouts out, "You should never hit anyone about God," and he jumps down gloriously into the firemen's safety net.

His words are like a sign from on high, having floated down to earth: "You should never hit anyone about God."

Roth means, of course, that in all sorts of ways, from how we're saved to how we observe Sabbath/Sunday to when and how Jesus will come again, we are still hitting people about God. When we insist dogmatically that our view is the only right view, we are hitting people about God. When strangers enter our churches, and we look at them askance because of clothing or ethnicity instead of harboring them, we are hitting people about God. When we condemn others for their deeds, without hearing their story, when we shun people with mental disorders and illnesses, when we fail to lay down our lives for this world Jesus loves, we are hitting people about God.

There is the link to a past of nearly two thousand years ago. The Pharisees, hearing of Jesus' miracle, swarmed to investigate its legality. They were, in their own eyes, God's SWAT team, the chief line of defense for the law. And they were forever ready to hit someone about God should they suspect a violation. Did they ever have a lot to check up on here, in this story of the man who had been blind!

First of all, a miracle occurred. Only God does miracles—they just don't happen. But, second, if a miracle *did* occur, it happened on the Sabbath, thereby violating the law. It takes a good person to work a miracle; only bad persons break the Sabbath. Third, the blind man was a bad man; his blindness was proof of it. Bad things didn't happen to good people. Yet, as the man himself argued, God doesn't listen to sinners. God listened to Jesus, so he must be a good man. By this time the Pharisees had had enough, so they just booted the man out of the synagogue.

Here is the irony of both the long ago past and also of the modern story. Jesus himself says it at the conclusion of the blind man's story, "If you were blind, you would not be guilty of sin; but now that you claim you can see, your guilt remains" (John 9:41). The Pharisees couldn't see beyond their laws. They tried to squeeze miracles into them and, afraid the whole structure would blow up in their sneering nostrils, kicked the man of the miracle out. No evidence, no grace. And the rabbi in Roth's story wasn't so different. The law reveals God. It reveals him as Almighty, Master of the Universe. But not as father of the miraculous Son of God. How to deal with it? Raise your voice and hit the rule-breaker.

Our blind man who teaches us to see truly, albeit without sight but with the heart, has still more to teach us about seeing the Messiah, however. And we may see that by comparing him to another biblical character, one who could see quite well physically, but didn't really learn to see until he was struck blind. His name was Saul.

Seeing the Light

We first meet Saul at the stoning of Stephen, the one who accused the people of having received the law but not having obeyed it. The people had ignored the prophecies fulfilled in Jesus; they liked the law just the way it was. They were guilty of a sin that still exists today: identifying God as the law he gave. They worshiped the law as if worshiping God himself, and thereby, in effect, made an idol of the law. They were deaf and blind to the God who spoke *through* the law.

A backdrop for Stephen's indictment rises out of the Old Testament, for the ancient prophets repeatedly accused the idolatrous Israelites, in their longing to have a god they could see and touch, of being deaf and blind to the living God. Isaiah, the prophet of the true and everlasting light, was particularly vehement in his denunciations of idolatry, and as he looked forward to the Messiah, he prophesied on the opening of deaf ears and blind eyes. In spiritual blindness people serve idols; in spiritual seeing they serve Jesus. "Lead out those who have eyes but are blind," said Isaiah, "who have ears but are deaf" (Isaiah 43:8). Such also was Stephen's message. But it did not fit the law. And Saul—a "Pharisee of Pharisees"—worshiped the law. There is a chill in Acts 8:1 with the words "Saul was there, giving approval to his death." Like a self-righteous, pompous judge he stood and watched Stephen die.

The death was incentive to Saul, and he believed his cause was a holy war. These people vilified the *law.* So he became the general in a war to eradicate the early church. He led the troops out in the field. He "dragged" men and women out of their houses, threw them in prison. Perhaps he was proud of his tally sheet—so many arrested equaled so many merits in service to the law.

Saul served the law with murderous fanaticism—until he took that trip down the road to Damascus and a voice from heaven pointed out his folly. As if in fulfillment of Isaiah's prophecy, the men with Saul were struck speechless. What can one say to the Lord's voice? Saul himself is struck blind by the light from heaven. What can one see when God reveals our own blindness?

Not all of us receive so stunning a road sign in our own winding paths of sin. We don't need to. We have the model of Saul before us. There is a happy end to Saul's story, of course. Miraculously his physical blindness is restored when his spiritual blindness is made whole. After receiving his sight, Saul became as zealous for Jesus as he had been for the law: "At once he began to preach in the synagogues that Jesus is the Son of God" (Acts 9:20).

The stories of these two blind men hold direction for us in our own watch keeping for the Messiah. For both, the Messiah had come, the long train of prophecies was fulfilled. We are positioned with them, guided by the prophets to the revelation of the Truth that is now a living presence in our lives. We too may "see" Jesus.

While the man born blind waited, hopelessly resigned to his condition, in his darkness and begging by the roadside, the other had a physical vision that allowed him to master all the sacred texts. Saul was a man of position, an intellectual powerhouse who studied with the best teachers and mastered languages. He was a leader in his intellectual circles. Yet he was as spiritually blind as the other man was physically. Until struck blind.

Here's the astonishing thing. Both were given sight. Both learned to see truly—not just with their eyes, however important that may be, but with their hearts. Here again are the words of the formerly blind beggar: "The man they call Jesus made some mud and put it on my eyes. He told me to go to Siloam and wash. So I went and washed, and then I could see" (John 9:11). And when the Pharisees pressed him, he simply responded, "Whether he is a sinner or not, I don't know. One thing I do know. I was blind but now I see!" (9:25). This is a testimony from his heart—a new life rooted in his heart and blossoming in his words to others. I was blind. I met this man called Jesus. And now I can see.

Nor is Paul's testimony any different once delivered from his spiritual blindness of idolatry. After "something like scales" dropped from his eyes, Paul rose up. For three days he had been down. For three days incarcerated in a grave of darkness. Now, on the third day, he rose up. And "at once he began to preach in the synagogues that

Jesus is the Son of God" (Acts 9:20). It was the same man named Jesus, the one who had healed the blind man, who had healed Saul.

Paul's approach differed, to be sure. He was a gifted intellect; the beggar had huddled alongside a road. Paul used argument and the law to prove his case; the beggar spoke from his heart. Yet the message was, and is ever, the same: This man called Jesus found me. Once I was blind but now I can see.

And so too it is as we keep watch for this man Jesus, the Son of God, yet today. Here and now, as Paul himself testified, "We see in a mirror dimly, but then face to face" (1 Corinthians 13:12 RSV). Paul well knew about seeing dimly, as if with scales over his eyes. So do we; it is our human condition before God.

What then do we do until we see clearly, face to face? In that same great chapter from 1 Corinthians, Paul provides his, and the Lord's, answer: love. Love is our way of seeing the kingdom of God fulfilled. Love, Paul says, never ends. Of course not; it is the living spirit of the most high and eternal God working through us.

However, this action of the heart is more often talked about than acted on in our age. More often we are aware of the struggles between powers and principalities that Paul speaks of. Some conceive of this in political terms, one party pitted against another. Some conceive of it in gender terms where one group has to obtain power no matter what the effect on the other. Or in ethnic terms where, again, hostile struggles for power rage out of control. And to all them, Paul, who once was blind and came to see, says, "Love."

But they are not words new with Paul. They are the words of this man named Jesus whom he met on the road to Damascus. They are words the blind beggar *felt* to the core of his being when he met that man named Jesus. For it is the word of the Savior himself. He said it like this: "A new command I give you: Love one another. As I have loved you, so you must love one another. By this all men will know that you are my disciples, if you love one another" (John 13:34-35).

We keep watch for Jesus. If we are to be found ready, excited to meet him, it will be by this great commandment he has given us: if we have loved one another. It is our own highest calling as we keep watch, no matter how brutal the battle beyond the ramparts of our souls may appear, no matter how dark the night in which we seek the light, no matter how long the days while we stare into an empty space. His love surrounds us.

So we keep watch.

For Further Study

Read John 9; Acts 9:1-20

1. The blind beggar is found by the pool called Siloam, which means "sent." What significance does that name have for the beggar? Or for us? Could we say that the very place where we are at this moment is a Siloam?

2. Another clear implication in the story of the blind beggar has to do with where the Pharisees and worshipers *were* and where Jesus *went.* What lessons emerge here for us?

3. How does the blind beggar testify to what happened? What lessons emerge here for us? Do you see a conflict between doctrinal theology and personal experience? How does that relate to Paul, who was himself a Pharisee, well bred in the doctrines of the day? What was his ministry like *after* his conversion?

4. A world of difference separates the beggar from Paul before their conversions. Name a few distinctions. But, more important, how are they similar following their conversions? How does this challenge us in the way we see others in the church?

5. How does the example of Philip Roth's short story mirror some of our actions in the church today? While we would agree that we need a fundamental purity in church doctrine and that certain things are nonnegotiable, what might be some ways in which we are still "hitting people about God"? What things seem to be nonnegotiable?

Prayer

I confess that often my eyes are dazzled by the bright, neon glitter of this world. I am bombarded by images of things I want. In wanting them I often blind myself to what you want for me, Lord. Open my eyes in the quiet stillness of searching for you so that I may see wholly and truly your way for me. Amen.

Conclusion
EVE, MARY &
THE LADY

---

*T*HROUGH EVE WE RECEIVED THE PROMISE, BUT AT WHAT A COST!

Imagine the heart of Eve as she walked away from her garden, never to see flowers with that particular boldness and beauty. It must have been a surprise of light and color at every turning, with foliage so lush that she could hardly remember its dew-draped beauty as she wandered east of Eden.

But what bowed her shoulders and pressed on her heart like cold fingers was nothing physical. It was something she could hardly name for it was altogether new in this world. It was a twofold loss of innocence and intimacy that made her shiver as she walked the dry land. That two-sided sword ripped a hollow in her heart.

I imagine that God's prophecy itself lost meaning under the daily parade of that loss. Who cared about crushing the serpent's head? She wanted her garden back. She wanted to talk with God, to tell him how she wished she had acted differently. She wanted to be held in his arms as she cried. She wanted . . . heart healing.

Forever after, Eve was haunted by those words, "If only . . ." But she couldn't go back and relive her past, doing things the right way. A flaming sword protected the Garden now, and all the pathways were blown over with ashes.

It is ever so hard to walk in the footsteps of Eve, but many of us—far more than we suspect, probably—do. The difficulty of plodding foot by foot in her dusty pathway is that we feel empty within and alone from without. Like a hollow chant from the recesses of a cave, we hear those words, "If only . . . if only." But it can't be undone.

I sometimes wonder what Eve and her helpmate Adam did that day they walked away. Were there angry words, faces set grimly toward the rising sun? Tears? Questions? "Where do we go?" "What do we do?" Because, for the first time, they were homeless, and they had to labor for their very lives.

As their anguish lessened, then came the time to question what God had meant by his words to the serpent, "He will crush your head" (Genesis 3:16). Who was *he?*

Apparently this person would be more than avenger; he would defeat the serpent—slay the death bringer. Maybe he would even bring hope to the disconsolate heart of those wandering east of Eden.

Eve and Adam had to walk away. With each step the memory grew dimmer. Can there be any doubt that the Lord was merciful? He did not abandon them utterly, either in the promise he made or the care he gave. He was still their God. So we assume that in time they found another home—but it could not match their one in the garden. And we assume they found measures of gladness returning in their lives—but it was not the former happiness of innocence. We imagine and assume this because, even as they trod dusty roads, they had been given a promise.

Centuries later, another couple, Mary and Joseph, walked *toward* fulfillment of that promise.

We may imagine that Palestine road was just as dusty, but instead of gardens they saw only brush and stunted trees. Few gardens would be open to this ragged young couple—perhaps they could wander by the Mount of Olives, but they were in a hurry. The Maker of all gardens, the Maker of Eden itself, was about to be born. The one who made the promise would now come as the fulfillment of that promise—in a spectacularly unimpressive way—to Mary, on a donkey led by her husband, riding to who knows where in Bethlehem.

To remake the garden, God goes underground in human flesh. He literally belittles himself. But from this time and for all time forth he is remaking the garden.

It must not have seemed so to Mary and Joseph. Consider Mary, as Simeon spoke words of disconsolation into her soul: "A sword shall pierce your heart also." As if she had not had enough to deal with. When would it stop? When could she rest and just be a mother?

But the sword did strike; and this was the way Eden began to be remade. By no other means could it be accomplished.

Again the dust blew. Again a pilgrim slogged foot by weary foot through the Palestinian dust, slowly climbing uphill. Then the miracle-worker, the Promised One, worked the greatest miracle in the only way he could. By the power of his miracles he brought others to life. By the miracle of who he was as the Son of God, *he brought himself to death.* The sword in the heart enacted the promise—and the restoration.

In his poem "Upon the Bleeding Crucifix," the seventeenth-century poet Richard Crashaw captures Christ's act. Here are the first and last stanzas:

> Jesu, no more! It is full tide.
> From thy head and from thy feet,
> From thy hands and from thy side
> All the purple Rivers meet. . . .

> This thy blood's deluge, a dire chance
> Dear Lord to thee, to us is found
> A deluge of Deliverance;
> A deluge least we should be drown'd.
> Ne'er wast thou in a sense so sadly true,
> The WELL of living Waters, Lord, till now.

The river of life, as Crashaw has it, flows from Calvary. It fulfills the promise by the Promise Keeper. Yes, but there is more. For any garden, and especially one of such lushness that it is named Eden, needs flowing water. The restoration is underway. But to where does it lead?

The Promise Keeper brought hope; hope first of all in our re-creation and second, in the re-creating of this world that was twisted after Eden (Romans 8:18-21). What do we hope for? Those very things lost in Eden: innocence and intimacy. Surely we receive some measure of them in this life; too often they are glimpses of grace that leave us begging for more.

Sometimes we seem to be kneeling like Job, in the dust east of Eden, bereft of any hope. Like him, we find no overflowing river of grace, but instead our "groans pour out like water" (Job 3:24). Job joins that chorus of human lament with others we have examined in this study, each keeping watch for promises to be fulfilled, for hope to be renewed.

And what of us? Having received the Promise Keeper, where do we fix our eyes in a world where we but see in a mirror dimly? We look ahead, for the Promise Keeper isn't done with us yet. His river, as Richard Crashaw put it in his poem, continues to pour down from Calvary, but to where does it flow? Its stream floods our hearts, washing and renewing, but where does it direct our lives?

The river flowing from Calvary, Crashaw points out, is the deep arterial flow of life's essence. This is Jesus' blood, poured out for us. The New Wine. It leads to the shining sea of crystal—our new hope where all things shall be made new, where the intimacy and innocence of Eden are reborn and everlasting. Consider the telling in the book of Revelation.

Final Warfare and the Lady

The book of Revelation was written during a time of fierce oppression of the young Christian church. Hope was battered under the fist of Nero. The stories that were whispered around the churches were not of doctrine but of gruesome atrocity. In the middle of this turmoil,

John received a revelation far more earthshaking than the present events, for he saw a time when the earth will literally be shaken apart and remade.

The book begins with charges to seven regional churches, then turns from earthly matters to divine matters as it pictures the Lamb on the throne. All heavenly hosts proclaim glory and honor to him, then the Lamb opens the scrolls of last things as the angels reveal them to John. Just after John sees the sacred temple opened (Revelation 11) with its revelation of the Messiah reclaiming his fallen creation, he witnesses the beginning of the last battle for that kingdom (Revelation 12).

At about this point I would expect to see the mighty armies of heaven arrayed—the flashing might of vanguards of angels, the brilliance of shining swords, the mighty leaders, ready to ride in power, scouring the earth of evil. This is standard operating procedure for any military operation, after all. Lead with an overwhelming display of might, put fear in the hearts of the enemies, and you have half the battle won.

This is what I would expect, but Revelation 12 opens with . . . a lady. And more, she is called "a great and wondrous sign." This Lady bears scrutiny.

Two things have to guide our understanding. First, as a "revelation" or vision of divine things, this revelation to John transcends time as we know it. It is eternal time seen through temporal eyes, timelessness with time-bound vision. In a sense the war in heaven has been waged since Satan was cast out of heaven, probably an event that preceded time as we know it. But also events on earth, such as the birth of Jesus, have huge implications not just for our time but for eternity. The result is that we have to partially suspend our reliance on the wristwatch and the calendar here. Second, if temporality is suspended to understand the events, then too the Lady can signify several time-bound women.

Several interpretations of the Lady have been advanced, each with a certain degree of credibility. Revelation 12:1 describes her as "clothed with the sun, with the moon under her feet and a crown of twelve stars on her head." Some relate this to David's description of God in Psalm 104:2. Others describe it as a fulfillment of female Babylonian deities often imaged in the same way. Some see her as the angel of the twelve tribes of Israel, or, indeed, as Eve—the mother of humanity.

But as we read further, we notice that this wonderful Lady, clad in light, is also pregnant. She cries out in labor pains (v. 2), and the "enormous red dragon" tries desperately to prevent the birth. Nonetheless, she delivers a baby boy "who will rule all the nations with an iron scepter" (v. 5) and who is snatched by God up to his throne. The woman has to flee into the desert.

Although there are anomalies in the time order, the spiritual significance of Mary giving birth to the Messiah stands out. We moderns spend little time reflecting on the spiritual warfare that accompanied the birth of Jesus, almost always looking at it only from the temporal, human point of view. Even from that point of view, however, we witness the long, dusty journey to Bethlehem, accompanied every step of the way by the scent of scandal at this illegitimate birth. We see the fury of Herod and the slaughter of the innocents. We see Mary and Joseph and Jesus fleeing for their lives into the desert toward Egypt. What we fail to see is the warfare in heaven as the spiritual battle lines are being drawn.

The Lady bore a son, that is the main thing. Out of humanity's failure to keep faith God gives a promise. Out of humanity's brokenness, God gives a hope.

The Promise Keeper wages the final war in heaven.

In Revelation 19 he appears as the one who is called Faithful and True, riding on a white horse. In our failure to keep faith, he is ever faithful; in our brokenness, when the brittle clay of our best efforts cracks, he remains true. And he is a warrior. Eyes blazing with fire, he goes forth to claim his bride. The armies of heaven are arrayed behind him, dressed in garments of gleaming white. His warfare imprisons Satan; it creates a new heaven and earth.

At the very heart of that new heaven and earth is no longer the arterial flow of the dying Christ. No, not anymore the keeping watch, the walking in deep and dark places of the soul. Here is "the river of the water of life, as clear as crystal, flowing from the throne of God and of the Lamb" (22:1-2). By this river of light, by the Sea of Crystal there will no longer "be any curse," and there "will be no more night."

The Lady of Revelation 12 gave birth to a Son that changed the currents of history. Here time and eternity intersected. Eternal God put on temporal being; temporal flesh was eternal God. But if eternal, he is now and ever present. Not some mythic figure lost in the ashes of the past, he lives and reigns with us.

I am "the bright Morning Star," Jesus says at the conclusion of the Revelation. Into the weary west the darkness is fleeing, its power, dug like claws into the land, being pushed backward. The darkness knows its defeat, even as the claws stretch to rip others into its maw. It is conquered. When Mary kept watch on Golgotha, she saw the sword pierce her son's side. She felt the sword of sorrow in her own heart too. What she didn't see is what the Lady saw—the sword in the heart of the beast.

Where does that leave us who still keep watch? We keep watch for the Holy City, surely. That place described in Revelation 21 where there is peace aplenty, where joy reigns. We keep watch for the bright Morning Star, to be sure. For if we know he has conquered, we know that we will not be conquered. By his river of life we are washed clean of even our darkest moments. But, as important as any of these, we keep watch for his presence right now, right here. Jesus, the all-powerful conqueror and the bright Morning Star, has also said, "I will not leave you desolate; I will come to you" (John 14:18 RSV). He is God with us, and God in us—the God of peace.

We too, like Eve, often wander east of Eden trailing a wake of broken fidelities. Sometimes we feel our faithlessness like stones upon our backs. We seek a promise for their removal.

We too, like Mary, can find the Promise Keeper growing inside our inmost being. The miracle of the Incarnation continues with the

Promise Keeper entering and directing our lives. Out of our brokenness he knits the pattern of new life.

We too, like the Lady in John's far-seeing vision, look ahead to the final conquering by the Lamb and the eternal reign of the bright Morning Star. Why, sometimes if we listen closely, it almost seems that we can hear the tremors of those far-off celestial hoofbeats and the blasts of the trumpet. We realize it is not so very far off at all.

For the Promise Keeper has kept all of his promises before; there is only this one yet to come.

While We Wait and Keep Watch

As we wait for that great Revelation, we carry each other's burdens, sharing the load as we travel through life. Sometimes our helpers can arise from the most peculiar sources. Perhaps one example will remind you of someone who has lightened your load in some way in the past, or maybe challenged you to help lighten someone else's.

I'll call this person Rita. And we should get this straight right away: she is no radiant angel of mercy, this Rita. I can't give you her home address either because she doesn't have one. Rita is a slovenly, loud, aggressive, openly lesbian woman somewhere in her thirties. (She isn't exactly sure of her age.) She is one of those persons who, whatever their place in life, wants to take immediate control of the situation. When Rita steps in—this short, squat, overweight woman— others step aside.

We first became acquainted with her through my wife, Pat, who volunteers as a nurse at an inner-city health clinic that ministers to the homeless. The streets around that clinic have a dark side. They can turn mean and violent in an instant—just what happened one day to Pat. As she walked across the street toward the parking lot after work, two thugs suddenly stepped up close to her.

"Hey. We need some money. Some money for a bus ride."

Pat was thinking of her key ring with the Mace spray. She almost always carried it in her hand. This time it was still in her purse. The two men drew closer. The streets seemed suddenly, desperately, empty.

Except for one person. Rita had been standing in a storefront, watching. In a moment she was out there, wedging her body between Pat and the two men, her loud voice shoving the men back like physical blows: "You gotta problem? You leave her alone! She's all right! Don't you ever bother her. You hear me!"

The two men turned and walked quickly down the street, their slouching walk not disguising their nervousness at all.

That's not the end of the story about Rita. If that were all, we'd have little more than a neighborhood bully protecting her turf. No, there's more to Rita, as another incident shows.

It was one of those autumn days when the temperature slides down and the rain pelts on gray streets. There is nothing quite so cold as wet cold; probably that is why Rita stopped in the clinic—just to get warm and have a cup of coffee. And so it was that while the staff went on with its always pressing work load, working with a jammed and noisy lobby of clients, Rita was the first to notice him, standing across the street in the rain at the bus stop. He was a young schizophrenic man who had been at the clinic for his medications. He was now waiting for his bus, and he stood soaking wet from head to foot. Suddenly Rita was across the street. She took off her own coat and placed it over the head and shoulders of the shaking man, and she waited there with him, her thick arms around him to keep him warm, until the bus arrived.

Will you think, just for a moment, of the woman who poured out her alabaster cruse of oil on Jesus' feet?

I know of one other story about Rita. On this day Rita was presiding with all the authority of a matriarch over the clinic waiting room when a new family entered. Rita saw their nervousness, their embarrassment. She went over to introduce herself to this hungry and homeless family, then suddenly left the clinic. She returned soon, carrying a large shopping bag containing a canned ham, bread and fruit. As she handed it over to the mother, Rita admonished her in the way of the street: "Now you find a place to eat this—feed those kids. Don't you dare sell it on the street for anything else." And she left.

It was an item of speculation for some time in the clinic just how and where Rita had gotten the groceries. Finally they simply agreed that Rita had her own curious ways and means. What mattered was what she did with what she had. She had so little but gave so much. And she gave impulsively, as if she couldn't help herself.

So too it is with us. On this side of the Incarnation we still wait for the Savior. With all those others in this book, we also keep watch for his coming. But waiting and keeping watch are not passive things. We seize every moment from this earth's kingdom for the coming of the Great King. We wait by helping the weak, the poor, the downtrodden, growing closer to that final revelation of glory. Waiting in such a way, keeping watch in such a way, we can almost hear the far off hoofbeats of the armies of heaven. They rumble closer every moment.

And as that moment approaches, and we keep moving on, one day when we least expect it, in the twinkling of an eye, the watch will be over—the trumpet will sound.

For Further Study

Read Matthew 25:31-46; Revelation 12

1. A conclusion is in many ways also a beginning. It is a time to take inventory and say, "Where do we go from here?" As you reflect on this book as a whole, what lessons do you take with you?

2. How can you implement these lessons in your life?

3. What comfort and guidance does this concluding chapter give us?

4. Is the idea of spiritual warfare a frightening thing to you? What brings you comfort?

5. Read Revelation 22. How does this passage respond to this entire study?

Prayer

Lord, I pray that I can integrate the lessons on how to wait for the Savior into my daily life—into who I am moment by moment. I thank you that the final victory is yours, and that while I wait here you have secured a place of eternal safety and joy for me with you. I look forward to that kingdom without end, without any trace of tears, where there will be no more waiting. Amen.